C000116062

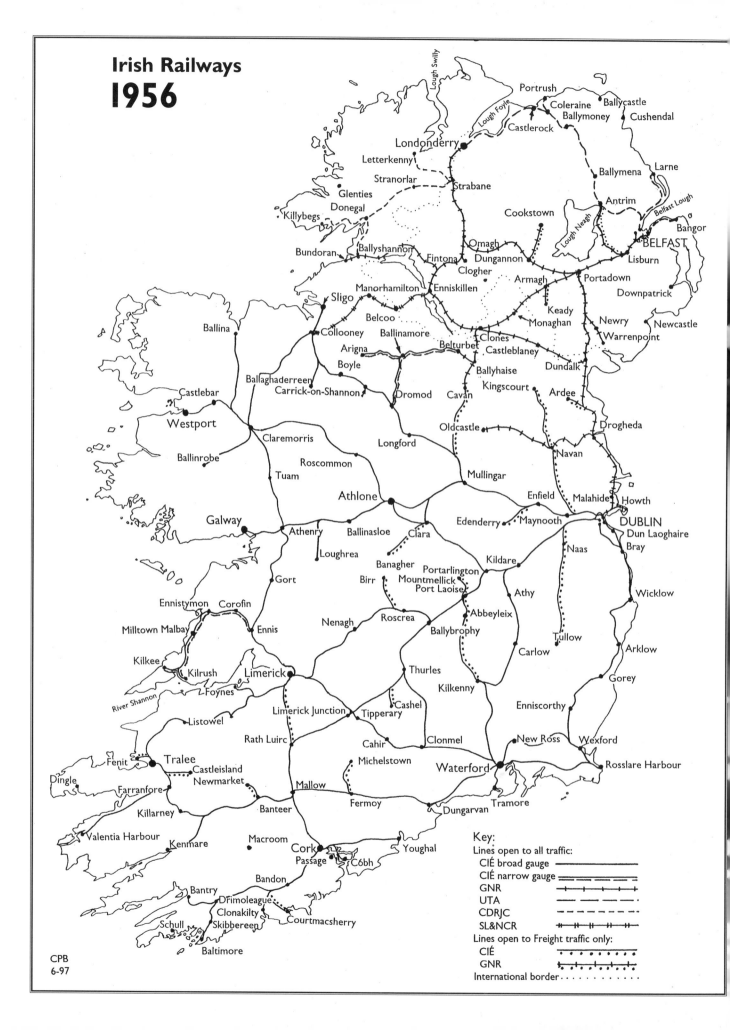

IRISH RAILWAYS

Forty years of change
1956-1996

Colin Boocock

Contents

Atlantic Publishers,
Trevithick House, West End, Penryn,
Cornwall TR10 8HE

First published 1997
© Colin Boocock 1997
ISBN: 0 906899 75 3

Layout and design: Richard Joy & Elizabeth Rodriguez, Paris
Jacket: Barry C. Lane, Sutton-in-Craven
Reproduction: Barnabus Design and Repro, Truro, Cornwall
Printed by The Amadeus Press Ltd, Huddersfield, West Yorkshire

All rights reserved. No part of this publication may be reproduced, stored in a retrieval system, or transmitted, in any form or by any means, electronic, mechanical, photocopying, recording or otherwise, without prior permission in writing from the publishers.
British Cataloguing in Publication Data: A catalogue record for this book is available from the British Library.

Dedication: This book is dedicated to my long-standing friend and

Previous page:The pride of the former NCC main lines were the class W 2-6-0 tender engines, most of which were named after rivers. In this view at Londonderry Foyle Road depot on 26th June 1963, W class No. 94 The Maine, which had been transferred to the GN section of UTA following the dismemberment of the GNR in 1958, poses with GN-type class S2 4-4-0 No. 62 Lugnaquilla. See Chapter 9 for the story of the GNR split.

Irish railway mentor, Dr. Donald McNeill. Not only did he encourage my early interest in things Irish, he greatly expanded my knowledge through the fruits of his own research, and today still sends me railway news from Erin's isle.

Photographs: All photographs in this book were taken by the author, except for the few that are otherwise credited.

Language: Throughout this book the initials for the railways in the Irish republic have been printed with their accents in position (e.g. CIÉ, IÉ), in recognition that the names are in the Gaelic language. However, the republic's name is normally expressed in English as Eire, without the Gaelic accent, and this convention has been used in this book.

Preface

Railways in Ireland have provided the author with as many surprises as have the people of that delightful land. In many visits spanning forty years, he has confronted new experiences that could only happen in Ireland. In 1989 he discovered a small book of Kerryman jokes in the bookstall at Dublin Heuston station. In it were lots of stories of the kind that the British tell of the Irish. Indeed many of them were the same jokes, but told by Irishmen about people from the county of Kerry. But it is the stories that come from Irish real life that are the best. Some of these appear in this book.

Wanting to tell people about the railways of Ireland and their idiosyncrasies, the author put together a colour slide show called Irish Surprises. This has been his most popular show, having been given to railway enthusiast groups over fourteen times. Indeed the Matlock Railway Club deserve special mention because they have seen it twice!

It was the railways of Ireland that first brought regular use of diesel railcars to the British Isles. Eire was the first country in these islands to abandon steam traction on its railways. It was the first to cease wagon-load freight traffic and to concentrate on trainload freight. It was the first to use decorative tiling on station concourses and platforms. It was also the first to introduce Commonwealth bogies to smooth the ride of its passenger stock. By contrast, Northern Ireland was the last part of the British Isles to stop using steam, and then for a time actually ran its railways with no locomotives!

Yet this is the island that produced the Fintona horse tram, and diesel railbuses converted from road buses. It kept ancient steam locomotives long

Above: *A lovely Irish railway anachronism was the horse tram that linked the GNR's Enniskillen-Omagh secondary main line with the town of Fintona just half a mile away. The mare Dick arrives at Fintona with the GNR tram No. 381 from Fintona Junction on 1st August 1956. The blue-and-cream liveried tram is now preserved in the Ulster Folk and Transport Museum at Cultra. Chapter 5 gives the Great Northern Railway background*

Opposite: *There is considerable excitement at Courtmacsherry station! Brand new Metro-Vick/Crossley 550hp Bo-Bo No. C232 has just arrived with an enthusiasts' special from Cork, formed of a short train of six-wheeled coaches. The year is 1957. This locomotive type replaced, for very few years, the tiny 0-6-0Ts that used to work this roadside tramway.* (Photo: T.J. Edgington/Colour-Rail)

after the U.K. railways would have scrapped them. It purchased the last clerestory coach to be built in Britain as late as 1926. It attempted to burn peat ("turf" in Ireland) in steam locomotive fireboxes. Eire really does fire several power stations on turf that is brought from the bogs on long trains hauled by tiny three-feet gauge locomotives.

The Irish railways do, even now, offer many surprises to the visitor from overseas. Apart from the wider rail gauge of 5ft 3in, there are high quality InterCity trains on the main lines, the very popular DART electric trains serving the Dublin Bay area, nippy Japanese diesel railcars in the south,

and the erstwhile "tub-thumpers", 4SRKT-powered diesel electric multiple units in the north. Clean trains and clean stations complement generally good time-keeping, except where heavy track renewals get in the way.

This book commemorates forty years of railway photography in Ireland. The book also expresses the author's delight at that lovely island. It is a medium for him to convey his thanks for the friendliness and help offered to him by Irish railway workers at all stages in his long railway journey. Please, enjoy this book, and then go there and see for yourself!

Colin Boocock

Introduction

In the nineteenth century, Ireland was part of the United Kingdom. However, the Irish built their main line and branch railways to the 5ft 3in gauge, not the standard gauge of 4ft 8½ in as in Britain. Many local railways in diverse rural localities were of the 3ft gauge, built to meagre standards at minimal capital cost.

Geographically, Ireland is quite unlike Britain. Many of its higher mountains and hills are round the edges, nearer the sea. The middle of the island embraces a vast acreage of peat bog-land. About 17% of Ireland's surface is peat bog. There are also some bogs found in the wilder areas of the far west, in Connemara and Donegal. The little railways that take milled peat to the power stations for burning are described in a chapter in this book.

With the capital city located about midway along the east coast of the country, virtually nowhere in Ireland is more than 250 miles from Dublin as the crow flies. The longest single train journey is from Dublin to Cork (166 miles). After the last war, for a short season of two or three years, the Belfast-Dublin 'Enterprise' train ran through to Cork making possible a through journey of some 279 miles.

The railway maps show clearly how most main lines radiate out of Dublin. Cross-country journeys were still possible as recently as 1960. The heavy railway closure programme eliminated the long link line, the former Waterford, Limerick & Western Railway. This single track stretched north-west from Waterford, via Limerick, by-passing Galway and eventually ending up in Sligo. From there the Sligo, Leitrim & Northern Counties Railway (SL&NCR) trundled even more slowly across the national border between Eire and Northern Ireland to reach the Great Northern Railway's secondary main line at Enniskillen. Other routes crossed and re-crossed the border, which follows county boundaries, not natural watersheds. But now, only the Belfast-Dublin line crosses the border.

As in Britain, the many individual railway companies in the Irish Free State amalgamated, this time in 1924 and 1925, to form the Great Southern Railways (GSR). In the North the Midland Railway and then the LMS owned most of the railways in Ulster through their Northern Counties Committee (NCC), except for those railways that crossed the border.

Apparently for political expediency, railways that crossed the border kept their relatively separate identities. The Great Northern Railway linked Dublin with Belfast, Londonderry and Bundoran. The County Donegal Railways' narrow gauge network (jointly owned by the NCC and the GNR) ran its geranium-red trains until it closed in 1961. The SL&NCR

Above: *The Great Northern Railway's passenger locomotives included some very handsome machines. This is C. Clifford's class S2 superheated 4-4-0 design that was built from 1913 to 1915 to haul heavy trains of ten to twelve coaches on the hilly main line between Belfast and Dublin. In striking blue livery, lined out in black-and-white, and with red buffer beams and valances, No. 190 Lugnaquilla is being positioned over an ash pit at Belfast Adelaide depot on 31st July 1956. The net on the side of the tender was part of the automatic tablet changing apparatus, used when the locomotive was working expresses on the Belfast-Londonderry route.*

Top Left: *While Ireland was still a poor country, the railways built to open up the more remote parts were often narrow gauge, normally 3ft. Ireland's first superheated narrow gauge engines were the class 5 2-6-4Ts of the 3ft gauge County Donegal Railway. No. 5 Drumboe, built 1907, waits on 1st August 1956 to start a freight away from Stranorlar, bound for Strabane. These locomotives were painted geranium red, and were also employed on summer weekend passenger excursions to the seaside resorts on the Ballyshannon branch. They had to take trains of eight or more bogie carriages up the gradients over the Barnesmore Gap, a test of the good pulling power of these competent machines. Chapter 6 refers.*

Left: *Main line locomotives in Ireland were often quite small. M. Atock designed some excellent little 2-4-0 express engines for the Midland Great Western Railway that were delivered between 1893 and 1898. The G2 class worked trains such as the Galway mail trains up to the last years of CIÉ steam. No. 665 was photographed at Bray on 6th August 1956 working a horse box train in connection with racing on the August bank holiday.*

survived until the GNR connection at Enniskillen was severed in 1957 by the GNR line closure. The Londonderry & Lough Swilly Railway closed before the author got to Ireland, as did all the 3ft gauge NCC lines, and several of those in the south. The massive cut-backs in the early 1950s reduced the Belfast & County Down Railway (B&CDR) to just the Belfast-Bangor section.

The Irish government nationalised the GSR in 1945 to form part of the national transport company Coras Iómpair Éireann (CIÉ). NCC and the B&CDR became part of the nationalised Ulster Transport Authority (UTA) in 1949. Still the cross-border lines remained untouched by the politicians. It was only when the GNR declared itself imminently bankrupt in 1958 that the two governments agreed to dismember it. They split its territory and assets as evenly as possible between UTA and CIÉ, the boundary being at the border crossings (see chapter 9).

In the past, the railways in Ireland offered more variety if less colour than they do now. Wherever one travelled, one would come across some unexpected oddity that the average Briton would not have seen at home. The years following separation of the Irish Free State (later to become Eire) from the United Kingdom were years of severe lack of money for capital investment. The railways were starved of cash, and only began to receive significant government funding for asset replacement in the early 1950s. Thus when the author first went to Ireland in 1956, there were still many locomotives from the nineteenth century in service. In addition there was a wide variety of types from the early years of the twentieth. The variety included some truly venerable

Above: *Another generation of Irish trains is now entering service in the 1990s. A "Japanese Sprinter" and a DART suburban electric train illustrate the modern face of Iarnród Éireann's Dublin suburban services. On the right, two Tokyu Car Co. two-car diesel multiple units, led by car 2612 delivered in 1994, head through Connolly station en route to Pearse to take up an afternoon peak working to Dundalk. On the left, a pair of two-car electric units pauses on a Howth to Bray working. The date is 24th March 1995.*

Opposite: *Full dieselisation came sooner to Eire than it did in Great Britain. Under a pall of incomplete combustion from its two-stroke 1,200hp Crossley diesel engine, CIÉ Metro-Vick Co-Co No. A25 starts away from Cork Glanmire Road station with a Sunday morning excursion train on 5th August 1956. This sharply curved main line station serves Eire's second city. Chapter 2 covers the early CIÉ diesel story.*

clerestory carriages, some on six-wheeled bogies. It was in Ireland that the author first rode in six-wheeled stock. The step change that then took place in Eire eliminated steam traction by 1964. (This was the official date for the end of steam, but the author and his friend Alan saw no CIÉ steam working during a tour in the summer of 1963.) In contrast, in the supposedly richer Northern Ireland, then only just beginning to experience modern terrorism, steam lived on until 1970. This was admittedly on special spoil trains topped and tailed by 2-6-4Ts to help build a motorway.

The author's soft spot for Ireland is unquenchable. Its railways still bear some evidence of their British beginnings. Seventy years of separate development of Eire from the U.K. have, however, rendered the country foreign in a number of ways. To the

British ear, the noise made by the popular General Motors diesel locomotives is uncharacteristic of anything heard this side of the Irish Sea. But in Northern Ireland, English Electric 4SRKT diesel engines power all the multiple unit trains. These remind one of the former Hastings diesel electric multiple units and of the few remaining Hampshire and Oxted types that still work to Uckfield and to Ashford.

The author is now at an age that he remembers whole fleets of new locomotives and railcars being delivered forty years ago, which have just been replaced by another generation of traction. There is another wave of investment occurring in railways in Ireland. The future looks bright, if the two national railways can continue to improve their productivity and earn more traffic. ◆

1

CIÉ's steam inheritance

Great Southern & Western Railway

The mergers that produced the Great Southern Railways in 1924 and 1925 joined up constituent railways of different sizes, gauges and characters. The biggest by far was the Great Southern & Western Railway (GS&WR). GS&WR main lines linked Dublin (Kingsbridge station) with Cork, Waterford, Limerick and Tralee. Its branch lines filled in the gaps. Only the Cork main line and the Queenstown (later Cobh) branch were double track - the rest of the system was single track.

The GS&WR bequeathed to the GSR a typically British range of 4-4-0 passenger and 0-6-0 freight locomotives. Their Britishness was altered subtly by the wider placement of wheels and buffers due to the 5ft 3in track gauge, and by the use of a smokebox door dart ring replacing the more usual handle.

From time to time famous British locomotive engineers such as J.A.F. Aspinall, H.A. Ivatt and R.E.L. Maunsell undertook the role of chief mechanical engineer. Locomotives that Aspinall and Ivatt produced in Ireland outlived their designers'

later products built for the Lancashire & Yorkshire Railway and (British) Great Northern Railway respectively. Only one Maunsell engine survived from his very brief Irish period, the 0-4-2ST *Sambo* that shunted the works yard at Inchicore works, Dublin, until the beginning of the 1960s. The most numerous locomotive class in Ireland was the 110 examples of MacDonnell 0-6-0s that the GSR classified J15 *(1)*. The design was remarkably similar to the Ramsbottom DX class of the London & North Western Railway. The

railway put into traffic these highly successful and long-lived engines between 1866 and 1903. They were often much rebuilt later so that in 1956 and 1957 they presented several varieties to the author's camera. Later, engineers Bazin and Harty produced more modern versions in smaller numbers.

Beautifully proportioned Aspinall class D14 4-4-0s were still working secondary services in 1957. Some even worked then on Dublin area suburban services for which their 6ft 7in driving wheels were quite unsuitable. The author last saw the

Ivatt 2-4-2 suburban tank engines of class F6 working in the Cork area in 1956. Ivatt's much more numerous 0-6-0T engines shunted in stations and yards almost everywhere.

Engineer Coey later developed an excellent and ever-enlarging line of 4-4-0s and 0-6-0s. These worked most main line services until engineers Watson and Bazin provided 4-6-0s to displace them. The 4-6-0s were handsome two- or four-cylinder locomotives, used on the Dublin-Cork expresses until dieselisation displaced them on to heavy freight workings.

Midland Great Western Railway

The MGWR connected Dublin (Broadstone station) with Galway, Westport, Ballina and Sligo. All main and branch lines were single track except for double track between Dublin and Maynooth, and for the last few miles into Sligo. Probably the most useful early locomotives that the MGWR passed on to GSR and CIÉ were the Atock 2-4-0 tender engines. The author heard that one of these engines had hauled CIÉ's last steam train, the night mail from Sligo to Dublin! (That may be an

Above: *This scene in Cork illustrates so much of the character of Ireland in the 1950s. H.A. Ivatt class J11 0-6-0T No. 217 transfers stock from Glanmire Road yard to Albert Quay along the Cork city railways link through the streets of the city. The train is crossing a lift bridge over one of the docks on 15th July 1957 having just passed two cyclists, two Volkswagen "Beetles" and a horse with a cart laden with hay bales. The fireman holds the bell to warn traffic of the train's approach. Note the coal merchant's premises in the right background ("Best Steam Coal" - "the House Coal People") and the sack manufacturers on the left.*

Left: *J.A.F. Aspinall's competent class D14 express engines for the GS&WR were delivered from 1885 to 1895 and survived to the late 1950s, being finally displaced from local and suburban work by the advent of diesel traction. Thus these engines outlived the designer's later 4-4-0s on the Lancashire & Yorkshire Railway by a quarter of a century! On August bank holiday Monday, 6th August 1956, modified class D14 4-4-0 No. 62 brings empty carriages for the Bray line through Dublin Westland Row station. Note that the Dublin inner suburban area was signalled with searchlight type signals by 1956.*

Left: *H.A. Ivatt provided some neat, small suburban tank engines to the GS&WR in Ireland in 1892 to 1896. No. 33 was still available for traffic when seen at Cork CB&SC section depot on 4th August 1956, presumably at that time being used on the Clonakilty branch train, almost certainly its last regular duty. These engines had ceased working the Cobh branch on the advent of a diesel railcar set, and had recently also been displaced by the closure of the Cork to Macroom branch.*

Right: *In 1957 the Cobh branch was being worked by a three-car diesel railcar set and by this steam locomotive hauled train. J15 0-6-0 No. 140 was a superheated example of Ireland's most numerous class. In the clean external condition exemplified by Cork Glanmire Road depot, it leaves Cobh with the 7.00pm to Cork on 15th July 1957. The first carriage is a fine twelve-wheeled clerestory corridor vehicle, and the other three coaches are equally vintage.*

apocryphal tale.) There were also two almost identical classes of 0-6-0s from the same engineer, J18 and J19. These operated all over the system on freight and also on branch passenger trains. They survived to the end of CIÉ steam. The little J26 0-6-0Ts were also popular, and found employment more widely over the GSR network than just in the MGWR area. There were also some small and large 4-4-0s that had disappeared by 1957.

The one major impact that MGWR locomotive policy had on GSR and CIÉ steam working occurred in 1925. To mitigate unemployment in London after the first world war, Woolwich Arsenal produced kits of locomotive parts based on the South Eastern & Chatham Railway N and U class 2-6-0s. The MGWR,

followed by the GSR, assembled twenty-six locomotives in Broadstone works from such kits from 1925 to 1930. Their arrival in Ireland, just as the grouping was taking place, gave GSR a fleet of powerful mixed traffic engines capable of handling most passenger and freight trains on all its main lines. They soon spread their activities and became common sightings on former GS&WR routes as well as on Galway, Westport and Sligo expresses.

CIÉ closed Broadstone station, following which the services on the former MGWR routes then started back at the former D&SER Westland Row station. The MGW section trains then crossed the river Liffey on the overhead link line through Tara Street and called at

Amiens Street station, connecting there with the GNR before heading along the MGW freight line from North Wall Quay.

Dublin & South Eastern Railway

Only a few 2-4-2Ts, a couple of 4-4-2Ts, some 0-6-0s and two inside-cylinder 2-6-0s survived into late CIÉ stock from the Dublin & South Eastern Railway. One of the 2-6-0s is happily now preserved.

The Dublin & South Eastern Railway started south from Dublin Westland Row station, and also from a terminus at Harcourt Street. These two routes distributed commuters from the suburbs widely in the city. Both lines served or connected with the main route south through Bray, Wicklow,

Above: *With steam to spare, even though some is being lost around the dome joint, superheated J15 0-6-0 No. 108 has run round its Sunday morning train from Cork to Tralee at Mallow on 5th August 1956. The run-round operation included turning the locomotive on the depot turntable just north of the station! The vintage clerestory twelve-wheeler almost dwarfs the engine with its outside-sprung tender.*

Left: *When an 0-6-0 design gets too big for the track there is only one thing to do: add a pony truck! R. Coey class K3 2-6-0 No. 361 of 1903 was stabled at Mallow depot on 5th August 1956. These engines were the GS&WR's heaviest freight locomotives until the advent of 4-6-0s in the 1920s. On the right stands another Coey freight engine, one of his class J9 0-6-0s.*

Top Right: *The massive form of a GS&WR 1921-built J.R. Bazin 4-6-0 would not fit the meagre British loading gauge! Two-cylinder class B1 No. 502 was seen at Cork Glanmire Road depot on 5th August 1956 being prepared for a main line freight working.*

Arklow and Wexford to Rosslare Harbour. The railway operated boat trains from Rosslare to Dublin as well as a quite intensive suburban service into Dublin from Greystones, Bray and Dun Laoghaire (formerly Kingstown). In CIÉ days the suburban services started back at Dublin Amiens Street, crossing the Liffey and calling at Tara Street and Westland Row before setting off on the former D&SER route.

Waterford, Limerick & Western Railway

The long, straggly line that connected Waterford with Limerick Junction, Limerick, Ennis, Athenry and Sligo was home for a while to engineer J.G.

Robinson. He later came to fame through his locomotives built for the Great Central Railway in England. CIÉ inherited 4-4-0s, 0-6-0s and 4-4-2Ts of his designs. The author saw only one of his Irish locomotives, a 4-4-2T in terminal storage at Cork CB&SC depot in 1957. The GS&WR absorbed the WL&WR in 1902.

Cork, Bandon & South Coast Railway

From an almost isolated terminus by Albert Quay, a winding single track set off south west to reach the coast at Bantry. The main line threw off two branch lines to the south coast, one to Skibbereen and Baltimore, the other to Clonakilty. The Clonakilty branch also connected with a road-

side tramway known as the Timoleague & Courtmacsherry Railway (could there ever be a more delightfully named railway?).

The mainstay of the CB&SCR fleet was a group of six Beyer Peacock 4-6-0Ts, four of which were superheated. Together with some D&SER and GS&WR 2-4-2Ts in CIÉ days, the 4-6-0Ts handled the heavier passenger and freight trains on the main line. The road-side tramway was of very light rail and needed engines of very light axle load. A small inside-cylinder 2-6-0T called *Argadeen* and some tiny GS&WR 0-6-0Ts sufficed for the meagre traffic on offer (until dieselisation, when C class Bo-Bos appeared for a short span!).

Great Southern Railways

Formed out of the amalgamation in 1924 of the GS&WR, MGWR, CB&SCR and several narrow gauge lines, and the D&SER in 1925, the GSR emerged at a time when investment capital was virtually non-existent. The greatest impact the GSR made on the locomotive scene was undoubtedly the construction at Inchicore works of Ireland's largest locomotives, the class B1a 4-6-0s designed by E.C. Bredin. Nos. 800-802, named *Maedb*, *Macha* and *Tailte*, were three-cylinder express passenger 4-6-0s, larger than LMS Royal Scots and little smaller than GWR Kings. Their appearance in 1939 was aimed in particular at speeding up the Dublin-Cork mail

Left: Although R.E.L. Maunsell served some time in Ireland, he did not design any main line locomotives while there. However, his N class 2-6-0 design for the South Eastern Railway in Britain was successful enough to be selected for building "on spec" at Woolwich Arsenal to relieve post-war unemployment. Twenty-six kits of parts were purchased by the MGWR and GSR. The kits were assembled at Broadstone works, the first locomotives being put into service in 1925. They served all over the GSR and CIE main line system. No. 396 was a 1930-built, 6ft wheeled version classified K1a, and was photographed at Broadstone shed, Dublin, on 3rd August 1956. The earlier engines with 5ft 6in wheels were class K1.

Left: *Like the GS&WR, the MGWR also had lots of 0-6-0 goods engines, mainly of classes J18 and J19. They were built from 1876 to 1895 to the designs of M. Atock. No. 593 was one with superheater and Belpair firebox. It is seen at Claremorris on 18th July 1957 waiting to depart with the 6.55pm branch passenger train to Ballinrobe.*

Right: *This view of D&SER class J8 0-6-0 No. 444 shows the typical Irish dished smokebox door clearly. In addition to the centre dart ring and handle there are small clamps at the door periphery to reinforce air-tightness, though many of these are unused. In the left background is one of the two D&SER inside-cylinder 2-6-0s, probably the one now preserved, No. 461. Unusually, the 2-6-0 has no smokebox door perimeter clamps. This view in the unroofed roundhouse at Broadstone depot, Dublin, was taken on 3rd August 1956.*

trains. War time shortages caused by other countries' fighting in the second world war frustrated this aim, and these large engines rarely had an opportunity to show their potential. After the war, track was not in high speed condition. Things only really improved in the 1950s, by which time dieselisation was in full flood and the B1a class engines were relegated to heavy freight work. No. 800 is now a fine exhibit at the Ulster Folk and Transport Museum at Cultra, near Belfast.

Coras Iómpair Éireann

When the author first went to Ireland in 1956, the railways of CIÉ still exhibited signs of having been starved of investment. Much track was of light, short-length rail. Except in the immediate Dublin area, all signalling was semaphore. Main lines were generally single track with passing loops, except for the Cork main line, the Dublin suburban routes, and the Cobh

branch. Stations maintained full complements of staff. Trains carried mail and parcels, and indeed anything that customers wanted to take with them or send. The whole outfit was very labour intensive, a scene that usually leaves little or no money left for investment. It was difficult to dismiss people, and many individuals were retained with little or nothing to do. Others were transferred to distant depots, their duties forcing them to commute from their homes. The locomotive fleet was generally not in good condition. Inchicore works carried out overhauls on a selected few locomotives while the rest waited their turn, being nursed along by the fitting staff at their home depots. There were some clean engines at Cork Glanmire Road depot, but these were the exception.

There were some delightful carriages in use. Other than main line expresses which had new stock, most trains included just one modern

vehicle, usually a timber framed body on a steel underframe on Commonwealth bogies, but the rest were truly antiques. The photographs in this book illustrate six-wheeled stock, twelve-wheeled clerestory coaches and an assortment of older, gas-lit bogie vehicles.

There were very few steam locomotive developments under CIÉ management. The author knows only of two, both related to the possibility of burning peat ("turf") in locomotive fireboxes. O.V.S. Bulleid, during his stay at Inchicore as chief mechanical engineer, converted a GS&WR K3 class 2-6-0 with forced draughting and a water pre-heater to enable it to burn peat. His main contribution, however, was to develop a successor to his "Leader" experiment (the "Leader" class were six technically novel 0-6-6-0 engines that the Southern Region of British Railways scrapped, without completing construction of the last five). Mr. Bulleid's Irish "turf-

Top Left: *A truly modern three-cylinder 4-6-0 design emerged from Inchicore works in 1939 from the designs of E.C. Bredin. Nos. 800 to 802 were built for the Dublin-Cork expresses and mail trains. War time conditions prevented them from showing their paces. No. 800 was withdrawn and restored to GSR green for exhibition in 1955. It was therefore a great surprise to see No. 800 Maedb at Cork Glanmire Road depot on 14th July 1957. The desperate motive power shortage caused by the poor performance of the Crossley-engined A class diesels had resulted in No. 800 being commandeered for freight working in summer 1957!*

Bottom Left: *A wheel arrangement not seen on British Railways was the 4-6-0T. Beyer Peacock supplied a small number of such engines to the Cork, Bandon & South Coast Railway from 1906 to 1920. These worked the main line to Bantry and most of the CB&SC branches, both freight and passenger traffic, until the onset of dieselisation. No. 463 was one of the two surviving unsuperheated engines, and is seen in Inchicore works yard, Dublin, on 22nd June 1963 prior to scrapping.*

Above: *Mr. Bulleid never gave up! Under the premise that a modern turf-burning locomotive could help CIÉ's and Ireland's future, he continued his "Leader" experiments at Inchicore. The 0-6-6-0 peat burning locomotive No. CC1 was mechanically more sound than the Leaders, but there were doubts about the adequacy of the boiler design which had a central firebox flanked by two rectangular fire-tube barrels. No. CC1 was photographed on 22nd June 1963 stabled among condemned locomotives at Inchicore.*

burner" 0-6-6-0, No. CC1, carried a rectangular section boiler with central firebox and rode on two chain-coupled bogies. Within each bogie was a small two-cylinder engine driving a crankshaft, with its piston valves driven by rocker arms powered through geared shafting. The master of engineering innovation had learned most of the "Leader" class lessons. The advent of dieselisation put an end to the need for such a machine.

Coaching stock

Travellers in Ireland in 1956 were beginning to experience a quality of ride that had not been achieved on the other side of the Irish Sea. Lightweight Commonwealth bogies with generous lateral swing enabled the new carriages of the 1940s and 1950s to ride on relatively poor track without the hunting and swaying movements associated with more traditional British single and double-bolster bogies.

Around 1950 CIÉ purchased a series of wide-bodied all-steel corridor coaches from Park Royal in the U.K. These vehicles had 10ft 5in wide bodies, making full use of the Irish loading gauge and being over a foot wider than the standard British Railways mark 1 carriages that emerged from 1951. The Park Royals were higher density cars, suitable more for secondary and suburban use than for expresses on the main lines. For the latter duties,

Inchicore works produced a handsome fleet of corridor saloon and compartment vehicles, also on Commonwealth bogies. These were vacuum braked, as was all Irish stock at the time. Internally the coaches were lined with stained and polished timber. Seats were trimmed in a somewhat open weave cloth that did not wear well. These well-liked coaches were painted light green. They suffered only in that their bodies had timber frames with steel panelling, which later led to their early demise when their crashworthiness was proved to be lacking in accidents. The earlier Park Royal stock outlived them by a decade. ◆

Right: *Irish government policy for many years has been for official notices to be presented in both the Irish Gaelic and English languages. Typical of early CIÉ station nameboards was this one at Dromod on the Sligo main line, junction for the Cavan & Leitrim section.*

DROMAD
DROMOD

2

CIÉ: The first diesel wave

Prototypes

In preparation for the first wave of full dieselisation of Eire's railways, CIÉ embarked on two diesel prototype ventures. The most important of these was a pair of Sulzer-engined 915hp Bo-Bos with Metro-Vick electrical equipment that appeared in 1950 *(2)*. CIÉ numbered these locomotives 1100 and 1101. They entered traffic on the Cork main line, and were still in use in the 1970s. Indeed, one of them has been purchased for preservation recently. There were also five 0-6-0 diesel electric shunting locomotives of 487hp, built at Inchicore to the outside-framed, fly-crank-coupled pattern well established in the United Kingdom and which later became class D. The diesel shunting locomotives were used largely around the heavy freight yards surrounding Dublin, particularly at North Wall Quay.

Diesel railcars

Diesel railcars began to appear in large numbers on CIÉ tracks from 1953. The new railcars were based on the Great Northern Railway's fleet of Park Royal AEC engined cars that were in turn a modern development of the British Great Western Railway railcars. Each car had two vertically mounted 125hp diesel engines underfloor, driving through five-speed epicyclic gearboxes. They also

Below: *The earliest bulk purchase of diesel main line locomotives by any railway in the British Isles was the acquisition by CIÉ of the 60 Metro-Vick/Crossley 1,200hp Co-Cos in 1955-1956. The A class were all in service before the first diesel from the British Railways 1955 modernisation plan arrived in 1957. This view at Dromod shows No. A51 arriving with the 9.25am from Dublin Westland Row to Sligo. The coaches have steel clad, timber framed bodies on steel underframes riding on light-weight Commonwealth bogies. The Cavan & Leitrim section terminus was just beyond the rear of the main station building.*

Right *No. B114 was originally No. 1101, the second of the two Inchicore-built Sulzer/Metro-Vick 915hp Bo-Bo prototypes that appeared in 1950. It was photographed on 22nd June 1963 after overhaul at Inchicore works. On the left is an A class Co-Co in faded original silver livery, while on the right is a class C in the light green that was used for the locomotives' first repaints. This colour was similar to that of the two Sulzer prototypes until the more stylish 1960s black and gold was applied.*

Below: *Brand new Birmingham Railway Carriage & Wagon Co./Sulzer 960hp A1A-A1A No. B102 pauses at Mallow with the Sunday 12noon from Cork Glanmire Road to Dublin Kingsbridge on 5th August 1956. These twelve locomotives, introduced that year, utilised the power units originally intended for six large twin-engined express locomotives.*

Above: *A Dublin to Galway or Westport express takes the Athlone route at Mullingar, MGN section, on 24th June 1963. The faded silver paint has left the A class Co-Co unidentifiable! The first vehicle behind the locomotive is one of Mr. Bulleid's two-axle train heating vans finished in stainless steel. The remaining coaches in view are standard CIÉ-built express stock in the light green livery of the 1950s, except the buffet car which is in black and gold.*

had speed-change gearboxes associated with the final drives. These enabled the cars to operate at a higher top speed (70mph) and lower acceleration for main line express work, or a lower top speed (ca. 40mph) and higher acceleration for suburban and stopping trains. The railcars were well appointed with spacious, comfortable seating. Half of them carried steam heating boilers. They ran in three- or four-car sets, marshalled outside one or two ordinary locomotive-hauled coaches specially wired for through control. Livery was mid-green with black and yellow lining.

Diesel railcar sets had duties on most main lines. On the Cork main line they would be marshalled as eight-car formations comprising four power cars and four locomotive-hauled stock trailers, including a buffet car. Their 70mph maximum speed was adequate for the timings then in force. Railcars also appeared on main line trains to Limerick, Sligo and Waterford.

CIÉ's diesel railcar sets also worked stopping trains, generally marshalled as three-car units, on all routes other than the smallest branch lines. They virtually monopolised the main line of the

CB&SC section, the Limerick to Sligo line of the former WL&WR, and stopping trains on the Cork and Limerick main lines. The railcars covered some services on the Cobh branch, and were seen on Dublin suburban routes such as that out of Harcourt Street.

The Metro-Vick and Sulzer fleet

In 1955, delivery began of the 60 Co-Co Metro-Vick diesel electric locomotives with Crossley 1,200hp two-stroke engines. CIÉ designated these locomotives class A. Deliveries finished in 1956. There followed 34 small Metro-Vick/Crossley 550hp Bo-Bos, the C class for branch lines, aimed at eliminating the last of the steam locomotives. It may seem ironic that railcars were not used for the smallest branch lines, but in reality

Right: *Squeezing through the narrow cutting at the approach to Skibbereen is 550hp class C Metro-Vick/Crossley Bo-Bo No. C202. It is working a branch train on 15th July 1957 formed of two six-wheeled carriages and a van from Baltimore to Drimoleague where passengers would change for the d.m.u. on the Bantry-Cork main line.*

Below: *Diesel electric shunting 0-6-0 No. D302 was photographed after overhaul at Inchicore works on 22nd June 1963. These Brush/Mirrlees machines were designed to develop 487hp. They were used mainly in the freight yards at Dublin North Wall and Kingsbridge.*

BY THE EARLY 1960s the A class were becoming notorious. The author remembers arriving at Inchicore works in 1963. He told his guide there, a technical engineer, that he had travelled that morning on the boat train from Dun Laoghaire to Kingsbridge station via the Phœnix Park curve and a reversal, hauled by an A class Co-Co. "How did you know it was an A class?" the engineer asked. "You wouldn't have been able to see it for the smoke!"

Top: *During the Bulleid era at Inchicore, CIÉ designed and built two batches of neat, 400hp 0-6-0 diesel hydraulic shunting locomotives. The E class employed Maybach high speed diesel engines. No. E414 was shunting condemned steam locomotives in the yard at the west end of Inchicore works on 22nd June 1963.*

Above: *On the same day, Deutz 150hp diesel hydraulic 0-4-0 No. G616 was awaiting despatch from Inchicore after overhaul. These little locomotives found unusual use in the late 1950s in attempting to resuscitate freight traffic on ailing small branch lines such as those to Newmarket and Castleisland in the west.*

it was logical. These small routes ran a minimum number of trains, most of which were of mixed formation of, say, one or two six-wheeled coaches, a parcels van, and whatever freight wagons were on offer.

In parallel with the Metro-Vicks, twelve more diesel electrics appeared in 1956 from the Birmingham Railway Carriage & Wagon stable. Their origin was unusual. Previously, CIÉ had planned to build six very large locomotives of

1,830hp. In this design, two six-cylinder Sulzer in-line diesel 6LDA28 power units were to sit within each locomotive body, making a long and heavy locomotive design. When the project faltered, the railway stored the power units in a tram shed near Dublin for several years, and then used them after refurbishment, one at a time, in the twelve B class A1A-A1A 960hp locomotives numbered from B101 to B112. The former 1100 and 1101 later became B113 and B114. It is worth recording here that the entire fleet of CIÉ, Metro-Vick and BRC&W main line diesels all used the same design of Metro-Vick MV137CW traction motor.

CIÉ had planned that the 108 locomotives forming classes A, B and C would be sufficient to complete its requirement for main line diesel locomotives.

Desperate situation

The plan suffered from two unrelated events. Firstly, the Crossley engines began to behave badly. Apart from setting up vibrations that caused some adjoining carriages to bounce up and down on their springs (!), the engines themselves suffered lubrication and component stress problems. The author remembers seeing a large pile of bent connecting rods and smashed pistons in the yard at Inchicore works. Crankcases also suffered fractures. By 1960, more than 50% of the A class fleet was out of action for repairs or spare parts. The traffic situation was becoming desperate. At this time, CIÉ was still pressing for the elimination of the remaining steam locomotives.

The second event was the sudden acquisition by CIÉ in 1958 of all the GNR lines south of the border. Where were the diesels to come from, that would be necessary to replace the remaining GNR steam locomotives?

These issues are dealt with in subsequent chapters in this book.

Train heating and lighting

Apart from the two Sulzer prototypes, none of the first wave of new diesel locomotives on CIÉ was able to supply steam or electric power for train heating or lighting. Indeed, no locomotives with what the Americans call "head-end power" came on the Éireann scene until late 1994. Some gas-lit carriages still survived (sublime darkness in tunnels!), while the remainder used traditional generators' belt-driven from axles supplying under-slung batteries which in turn provided current for lighting. CIÉ built a number of four-wheeled, stainless-steel clad boiler vans for use with diesel locomotives, and these served this purpose for many years, as well as acting as guards' and luggage vans. They were wide-bodied, unpainted vehicles, and added to the variety of liveries in a CIÉ passenger train formed with dark and light green carriages and an aluminium-silver locomotive! The use of four-wheeled heating vans limited the future potential for raising main line speeds.

CIÉ also built a number of wide-bodied main line carriages with an unpainted stainless steel body finish at Inchicore for express services. One imagines that at that time there was a vision of an express train being of silver livery from end to end, but the numbers of such coaches never seemed to enable such a formation to be regularly achieved. ◆

Top: *The CIÉ Park Royal diesel railcars had much shorter lives than most of British Railways' d.m.u.s. Nonetheless they were popular with passengers, apart from a propensity to suck in diesel engine exhaust via the carriage windows. Railcar 2629 is part of a three-vehicle set that is reversing at the small intermediate terminus station at Newcastle West while working the 8.15am from Tralee to Limerick on 17th July 1957. The intermediate vehicle is a standard express carriage, wired for through control. Livery is mid green with black and cream lining. Some of these railcars ended their lives shorn of their traction equipment and running as push-pull trailers on Dublin suburban services.*

Above: *In 1957 Inchicore works built two additional diesel railcars on AEC underframes to augment the Park Royal fleet. No. 2663 was at Cork Glanmire Road depot being refuelled and serviced on 14th July 1957 before working on an express to Dublin. The train was formed of three railcars at one end, one at the other and four trailer cars in between.*

3

The coal and cattle railway - Cavan & Leitrim

Clanking slowly along the narrow railway track at the side of the winding country road, the ancient 4-4-0T was performing the once-a-day duty of providing the Arigna branch with its passenger service. The driver was worried. At the last two stops he had had to delay the train to attend to an overheating bogie bearing. "I can hear the empties following us," he said. He was referring to the empty train of nine wagons and a brake van that was a mile or two behind us on the branch. He heard the high-pitched whistle of the ex-Tralee & Dingle 2-6-0T again, probably as it approached a road crossing. The coal train seemed to be getting closer. I asked what means of separation there was to prevent trains on this single line catching each other up. "I've got the ticket - he's carrying the staff for the section. I am expected to stay ahead."

I resumed my perch on top of the pile of slack coal that covered the cab floor of 4-4-0T No. 2L. The unguarded water level gauge glass showed the water level to be well up over the top of the firebox. The vacuum gauge registered 15in of vacuum, the engine's vacuum ejector seemingly being unable to attain the intended 21in.

The engine rolled gently down a long hill with its one, old clerestory,

canopy-ended coach and a few vans behind it. The assembly approached a curve in the road where the track crossed the roadway obliquely, a high hedge obscuring the view of any approaching traffic or animals. The driver dropped the brake handle to its full-on position. Almost nothing happened! The train trundled slowly round the corner, across the road, and continued, admittedly more slowly, on the other side. Had

any obstruction been met, the locomotive would have hit it. Its cowcatcher would have had to prove its worth.

The Cavan & Leitrim section of CIÉ operated with a mixed fleet of 3ft gauge tank engines, most of which had been displaced from other narrow gauge lines that had closed. The route formed a capital 'T' on the map. The upright of the 'T' was formed by the "main line" from Dromod, where trains

Above: *An Irish antiquity still in operation as late as 1957 was the service of coal trains on the 3ft gauge Arigna branch on the Cavan & Leitrim section of CIÉ. For most of its length, the Arigna branch followed the public road from Ballinamore. This course led to steep inclines and sharp curves. On 24th July 1957, former Tralee & Dingle Railway Kerr Stuart 2-6-0T No. 4T had nine loaded coal wagons in tow passing the tiny halt at Cornabrone bound for Belturbet. There the wagons would be emptied manually by shovel, the load being transferred to 5ft 3in gauge wagons for the onward journey on the GNR.*

connected with the former MGWR line to Sligo. The cross-bar of the 'T' formed the Arigna branch to the west, and the continuation of the "main line" to Belturbet in the north-east. At the central confluence of these narrow gauge lines was the railway town of Ballinamore, a small, single street, lined on both sides by houses and a few shops.

Most Dromod trains were worked by 2-4-2Ts. These were relatively high-stepping machines, more suited to fast suburban work than to crawling over hills with trains of mixed passenger cars and cattle trucks. Four of them had come from the Cork, Blackrock and Passage Railway when that closed in 1934, and had been numbered

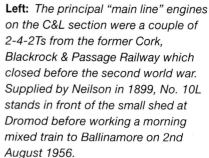

Left: *The principal "main line" engines on the C&L section were a couple of 2-4-2Ts from the former Cork, Blackrock & Passage Railway which closed before the second world war. Supplied by Neilson in 1899, No. 10L stands in front of the small shed at Dromod before working a morning mixed train to Ballinamore on 2nd August 1956.*

Top Right: *Cavan & Leitrim Railway 4-4-0T No. 3 was once named* Lady Edith. *On its final withdrawal from Irish service, No. 3 was taken to the USA and restored for exhibition. On 24th July 1957 No. 3L takes an empty coal train away from the junction at Ballinamore, bound for the Arigna coal mines. The C&L "main line" to Dromod is in the right background. It's good to see the safety valves lifting on a Cavan & Leitrim locomotive.*

Bottom Right: *Three of the former Tralee & Dingle 2-6-0Ts found their way on to the Cavan & Leitrim section of CIÉ when the T&D section was being run down. No. 3T, of a class originally supplied by Hunslet from 1889 to 1910, stands at Ballinamore with the most decrepit stock that the author has ever seen on a public railway passenger train. This was the Arigna branch train on 2nd August 1956.*

Below: *Former Tralee & Dingle Railway Hunslet 2-6-2T No. 5T also worked the C&L main line mixed trains. On 2nd August 1956 it was seen at Ballinamore, the junction station in the midst of the C&L system, waiting to leave with the 2.35pm to Dromod. Bracket bolt holes are visible in the deep buffer beam where the cowcatcher had been fixed. A cowcatcher was not required for the Dromod-Ballinamore-Belturbet "main line". This engine was later displayed in the USA for many years, and is now back in service on the Tralee & Blennerville Railway (see Chapter 16).*

"AS I CHATTED to the occupants of the station house at Arigna, the mother of the family there told me with utter certainty that when any of the Cavan & Leitrim engines broke down, CIÉ would sent them a replacement "from another old railway". I hadn't the heart to tell her that there were no more little railways left that had small enough engines. (The 4-6-4Ts and 2-6-4Ts of the County Donegal Railway were surely too big for the C&L.)"

10L to 13L in the CIÉ Cavan & Leitrim series, as witnessed by the suffix 'L'. The CB&PR had been a partially double-track line that linked Cork city with suburbs along the estuary to the south. Now the two surviving 2-4-2Ts were serving in an agricultural community, at a much slower pace. Their "main line" duties were shared with a chunky 2-6-2T that had come from the Tralee & Dingle Railway. This was No. 5T ('T' for T&DR in the CIÉ number series), which later went on display in a museum in the USA. The 2-4-2Ts and the 2-6-2T also worked to Belturbet on the mixed trains.

The principal group of former T&DR locomotives on the Cavan & Leitrim were two sturdy little 2-6-0Ts from Hunslet and one from Kerr Stuart. These normally worked the coal trains between Arigna and Belturbet. Coal was the staple freight that kept the railway going. The quarries at Dereenavoggy beyond Arigna supplied small coal that was transported by C&L train to Belturbet and Dromod. There, labourers shovelled the coal manually into broad gauge wagons for onward transit. Arigna was Ireland's only indigenous coal source.

The original 4-4-0Ts came from the Sharp Stewart stable in the 1880s. Originally, they had

performed all duties on the line, other than when a heavy 0-6-4T had been purchased, tried and proved to be too heavy. More recently the observer could only marvel at the manner in which the C&L fleet had been enlarged by transferring second hand machines from other railways while little money was spent on overhauling the indigenous fleet. Only 2-6-0T No. 6T appeared as an overhauled engine in post-war enthusiasts' collective memory.

The 4-4-0T on which the author was riding in 1957 clanked into the station at Arigna. Soon it was shunting gently towards the turntable. The empty coal train that had been chasing, passed round the junction at the side of the station and its driver handed over the staff, the 2-6-0T making good progress. The 4-4-0T gingerly stepped on to the turntable with its fireman driving. The near end of the turntable bridge dropped with a bang about four inches under the bogie axle weight. The driver stood alongside, watching the turntable like a hawk. As the engine stopped with the table in balance, the whole ensemble began to lean to the left. Both men carefully pushed the table round, the 4-4-0T listing precariously. The author was becoming even more concerned at the condition of this otherwise delightful railway. Even though all Irish narrow gauge lines mainly used tank locomotives, they adopted a standard practice of turning them at each end of each journey.

To the author, the line's future looked bleak. Its end came less than two years later, in April 1959, when a coal-fired power station was commissioned just alongside the Dereenavoggy mines. The railway was then no longer needed (3). ◆

4

The all-diesel narrow gauge line - the West Clare

Against the trend elsewhere, CIÉ made an effort to prolong the life of the 3ft gauge railway that linked Ennis with two small coastal towns on the edge of County Clare. The West Clare Railway (WCR) passed through a few villages and seaside watering places, but generally wended its way through a bleak and stony land. There were no large centres of population, and what agriculture there was had to eke its produce from infertile soil. It was little wonder that the WCR was impecunious.

The little railway had been immortalised by the poet, Percy French. We quote in part:

Are ye right there, Michael, are ye right?

Do ye think that we'll home before the light?

'Tis all dependin' whether the old engine holds together,

But we might now, Michael, so we might!

It seems that the line had been strapped for cash for generations! The injection of investment in new diesel rolling stock and locomotives that took place in the early 1950s must have seemed like a Godsend to the local railway people, and would certainly have boosted the locality's confidence in its railway.

In 1952, Walker Brothers of Wigan delivered four articulated diesel railcars to the WCR, to the same pattern as those they had supplied for many years to the County Donegal Railway (which are described in chapter 6 in this book). The railway provided trailer coaches, made of bus bodies adapted to fit on old carriage underframes. The railcars were unidirectional, and so needed to be turned at each journey's end. The old steam locomotive turntables were already there for the purpose.

Three diesel locomotives were supplied in 1955 for the useful freight service that the line enjoyed. They were also able to take on extra passenger workings when needed. These were B-B locomotives made up of two railcar bogies under a

Below: *There appears to be considerable activity at Ennis station, though it is probably fleeting, as Metro-Vick Co-Co No. A6 arrives with three coaches and a heating van forming the 12.45pm from Limerick to Galway. The 3ft gauge West Clare section connection, due to depart at 1.50pm for Kilrush, stands in the bay. The narrow gauge train is formed of Gardner-Walker diesel mechanical railcar No. 3387, one bogie coach and a four-wheeled van. The date is 17th July 1957.*

common frame, driven from a central cab. The two Gardner diesel engines gave each locomotive a power of about 200hp. The wheels were coupled with outside coupling rods (just like the railcars) which gave them good adhesion.

The line connected at Ennis station directly with trains on the Limerick-Galway and Sligo services. Leaving Ennis, the single track curved towards the west coast, calling at small towns such as Corofin and Ennistymon. At Lahinch there was a sight of the Atlantic Ocean as the railway, now heading south, ran along cliff tops, and then a little inland through rough country. The train clanked its way (yes, the diesel railcars' coupling rods clanked!) to call at Milltown Malbay where perhaps a freight would be crossed, and eventually came to a halt at a V-shaped platform, seemingly in the middle of nowhere, sign-posted as Moyasta Junction. Here, there was usually another, connecting railcar train waiting at the opposite face of the single platform, facing the same direction. The railway split at Moyasta, one branch heading west to the tiny seaside resort of Kilkee. The other branch headed south-east to Kilrush, a port on the Shannon estuary. The railcar that made the connection also provided a short-distance service linking Kilkee with Kilrush, so the local community was actually quite well served.

By the time of the author's 1963 visit to Ireland, the West Clare line had long been closed. The three B-B locomotives and a railcar cab unit were in the scrap yard at Inchicore works. Only one of the steam locomotives had survived, an 0-6-2T that ended up on a plinth at Ennis . ◆

Above: *Were it not for the rain, one can imagine that someone would be on the top of the station awning at Milltown Malbay repairing it! CIÉ introduced three of these B-B diesel mechanical locomotives using standard railcar power bogies complete with engines and transmissions. They were supplied by Walker Bros. of Wigan in 1954. No. F503 is briefly checked over by its driver while working the Ennis to Kilrush freight train on 18th July 1957.*

Below: *Walker Bros. railcar No. 3388 arrives at the small seaside resort of Kilkee on 18th July 1957 with the 8.45am from Ennis. The trailer carriage body uses road bus components on an older carriage underframe.*

5

Great Northern - the international railway

A confident railway

The image of the Great Northern Railway of Ireland that pervades through the mists of time to today remains, for the author, the sight of a bright blue VS class 4-4-0 at the head of a long train of heavy, golden teak corridor coaches. Other people may remember small, black PP class 4-4-0s with three brown non-corridor bogie carriages on some local stopping train meandering through the border counties. Still others may recall the smart blue-

Right: *Many connections were made at the GNR station at Clones from which railways went off in four directions. On 24th July 1957, 1948-built U class 4-4-0 No. 205 Down leaves with the 4.30pm from Dundalk to Enniskillen (left), a three car diesel unit awaits departure on the 6.30pm to Belfast Great Victoria Street, and [off right] PP 4-4-0 No. 106 stands with the 6.25pm to Dundalk. A train from the Cavan branch had previously arrived with PP No. 72, on a stopping service to Belfast.*

and-cream diesel railcar trains, or the variety of chunky, black 0-6-0s that persisted with the classic mixed freights made up of four-wheeled wagons and vans that must have seemed the same as those their grandfathers knew.

All will remark, to a man (or woman), that the GNR had atmosphere, that its staff were smartly turned out and attentive to their work, and that it was an effectively run railway with high standards of operation and cleanliness. To someone who had just travelled over the investment-starved broad gauge tracks of CIÉ in the 1950s, the GNR was indeed a pleasant railway to behold. The Great Northern also was not flush with investment money, but its management had been successful in making the best of what they had.

Above: *What gorgeous little 4-4-0s the PP class were! To the designs of C. Clifford, they were built from 1896 to 1911. Old No. 42 arrives at Strabane during a downpour on 1st August 1956 with the 8.18am from Omagh to Londonderry. Note the GNR clerestory coach in the middle of the train. The locomotive is black; the coaches are varnished teak. In the foreground is a dual gauge wagon turntable that was shared between the GNR and CDRJC.*

Top Right: *Clifford provided the GNR with a fleet of simple 0-6-0s of which the class PG were early examples being delivered from 1899 to 1904. These were based on the earlier class AL goods engines that had been designed by J.C. Park. Class PG 0-6-0 No. 10 stands in Enniskillen depot yard on 1st August 1956. The raised letter "B" on the cabside denoted a freight haulage power class which the GNR used; "A" was the lowest (class AL) and "D" the most powerful (including classes QLG and SG3).*

Bottom Right: *"Have bicycle, will travel!" Class RT 0-6-4Ts were used as freight shunting engines in the Belfast area, including the docks lines. No. 22 was the subject of the author's first photograph taken in Ireland, on 31st July 1956 as it performed near Queen's Quay*

Many of its locomotives and much of its rolling stock were old, but there had been steady, if slow, replacement of the oldest. The new steam locomotive designs were very conservative. This had the unusual effect of bringing, for example, brand new inside-cylinder 4-4-0s and 0-6-0s of the U class family into service for secondary routes as recently as 1948. Beyer Peacock had delivered in that same year five large VS class three-cylinder 4-4-0s for the Belfast-Dublin main line, which worked the

fast, non-stop 'Enterprise' expresses as well as other, heavier fast trains on the main line. These engines were named after Irish rivers.

fast, non-stop 'Enterprise' expresses as well as other, heavier fast trains on the main line. These engines were named after Irish rivers.

The VS class were in effect a simple version of the famous G.T. Glover 4-4-0 compounds of class V. The five compounds, which carried the names of fast-flying birds, were large, graceful machines. Each locomotive had one high pressure inside cylinder exhausting into two low pressure cylinders set on the outside of the frames, on the Smith principle. The wheels were quartered at 90° thus giving four exhaust beats a wheel revolution. Both groups of three-cylinder 4-4-0s were painted mid-blue with black-and-white lining, with red, deep buffer-beams and red valances. These engines were always clean. They exhibited the proud face of a confident railway.

Locomotive families

Older 4-4-0s that still had main line duties in the mid-1950s were the eight examples of C. Clifford's S and

Above: *A handsome design introduced by G.T. Glover for Belfast suburban duties from 1921 to 1929 was the 4-4-2T group classified T1 and T2. Class T2 No. 69 stands outside the shed at Belfast Adelaide depot on 31st July 1956. Note the unusual feature of brakes on the leading bogie. These locomotives had similarities to the U and UG family of GNR engines.*

S2 class inside-cylinder engines. These fine-looking locomotives were also in blue livery, and carried the names of mountains. They were externally almost indistinguishable from the black-liveried Q class, also by Clifford, that had been introduced in 1899. The S and S2 engines worked on the Dublin-Belfast main line. They also monopolised the Belfast to Londonderry expresses, and they worked the Dublin-Derry and Bundoran expresses as far as their reversal at Dundalk.

Clifford's earlier masterpieces had included the small and delightful PP class 4-4-0s, graceful, long-chimneyed engines that in the 1950s were still able to turn their wheels at over 60mph on secondary main line stopping trains. They worked most of the stopping trains

on the lines south of Derry, and were staple power on the more significant branches.

The PPs were very old by the end of the second world war, and replacements for some of them came in 1948 in the form of another batch of U class 4-4-0s, lightweight, blue-painted and named after counties. The original U class design dated back to 1915! One haunt of these pretty engines was the 'Bundoran Express'. They used to take this train over at Dundalk from the S or S2 that had brought the express north from Dublin, and worked it over the cross-country route through to Clones, Enniskillen, Bundoran Junction, Ballyshannon (where it made a tenuous connection with the County Donegal narrow gauge line) and the Atlantic coast resort of Bundoran.

The U class had freight and suburban equivalents. The UG goods 0-6-0s and the T2 4-4-2Ts (Belfast's suburban tanks) shared with the U 4-4-0s common boiler and cylinder dimensions. A common Clifford practice was to provide freight 0-6-0s that matched the passenger engines dimensionally. Thus, for example, the GNR had UG, QG, SG, and SG2 0-6-0s that were very similar to the U, Q, S and S2 class 4-4-0s. The largest goods locomotives were the handsome SG3s which came from the Glover era.

Railcars in service

In 1949 the GNR received the first of a series of diesel railcars from Park Royal. These were based on the popular Great Western Railway AEC cars, but were all designed to be operated as three-car or four-car sets in multiple. A four-car formation was put into service on the Dublin-based 'Enterprise' working, using locomotive hauled stock as trailer cars including a buffet car. Liveried in blue-and-cream, these trains looked good, and were a credit to the railway. Three-car sets operated Belfast to Londonderry, Belfast to Enniskillen via Clones, and some Belfast suburban services out of Great Victoria Street terminus.

The AEC cars were not the first to work trains on the GNR. A selection of small diesel cars had been in use on local and branch line workings for many years, including a couple of the Gardner-Walker articulated type favoured by some of the narrow gauge railways. The summit of development of the Gardner-Walker type was the group of four units which worked the Dublin suburban service from Amiens Street station to Howth. The first two of these had a central power unit on three axles with wheels coupled by side rods, a passenger car being articulated from each end of the central unit. The second two had a more conventional four-wheeled central unit with cardan shaft drive.

Even more basic were four diesel railbuses which were literally just that - single-deck road buses running on railway flanged wheels. Among them were wheels designed by a GNR engineer, that used steel tyres with pneumatic tyres inflated within them (the Howden-Meredith wheel). These railbuses worked sparsely trafficked branch lines like that from Drogheda to Oldcastle.

GNR trams

The outer two stations on the Howth branch each connected with a 5ft 3in gauge electric tramway. The Hill of Howth tramway was owned by the

Below: *The 'Enterprise' expresses used to run non-stop between Belfast and Dublin. In 1956 the train set based in the north was in its last year of steam haulage. Formed mainly of modern steel-panelled stock, albeit painted to resemble varnished teak, the formation includes a blue-and-cream buffet car near the rear. This buffet car (and the one in the diesel unit 'Enterprise' set that operated out of Dublin) used to carry two different bar cabinets, one for use each side of the border, due to the differing tax rates on drinks in either country. Class VS 4-4-0 No. 209* Foyle *worked the southbound morning train on 7th August 1956 and is seen approaching Dundalk station.*

GNR. Its double-deck trams climbed from Sutton station, turning south to gain the summit of the Howth peninsular, and then dropped down a steep gradient north-westwards to reach the railway again at the Howth terminus. Three of the trams survive in preservation today, one of them at the National Transport Museum at Howth which specialises in buses and tramcars.

The most basic form of railway passenger transport ever experienced by the author connected with GNR trains south of Omagh on the Enniskillen line at a small station called Fintona Junction. The branch line to Fintona was only half a mile long. It was serviced by a four-wheeled tramcar worked by a horse. Upstairs was third class; downstairs there was first and second class accommodation. When the GNR cross-border railway closure programme began in 1957, the Fintona horse tram vehicle was retired to the transport museum in Belfast; the horse, a mare called Dick, retired to an adjacent field. ◆

Above: *A lovely trip to do on balmy summer evenings was to take the Howth branch diesel train out to Sutton station and there board one of the GNR's 5ft 3in gauge electric trams for the climb to the summit of the Hill of Howth, from which fine views were to be had across Dublin Bay. Then the visitor could descend on the tram to Howth village itself for a meal and a leisurely return by train to Dublin. Trams 4 (left) en route to Howth and 2 heading for Sutton cross at the summit on 5th August 1956.*

Below: *For branch lines with meagre traffic the GNR used small railcars of various kinds, including a couple of converted road buses. Railbus No. 2 used to work the Oldcastle branch. It was seen at Dundalk on its purpose-built turntable on 24th July 1957. The rear wheels were pneumatic tyres inflated within steel flanged tyres, a type patented by GNR engineers Howden and Meredith. Some railbuses had all four wheels of this type.*

Above: *The GNR had a number of odd diesel railcars from the pioneering era, including this splendid affair, numbered A in the railcar series. This car had a single, 102hp diesel engine and is seen at Strabane in 1956.* (Photo: P.B. Whitehouse/Colour-Rail)

Below: *On the Belfast-Dublin main line, class QNG 0-6-0 No. 38 arrives at Dunleer with a southbound freight train in September 1958. (See Chapter 9 to explain the reason for the designation "CIE" on the buffer beam.)* (Photo: J.G. Dewing/Colour-Rail)

6

The big little railway - County Donegal

Geranium-red engines, tiny red-and-cream diesel railcars, long freights of grey four-wheeled and bogie wagons tailed by red-and-cream guard's bogie vans - what a charming picture the 3ft gauge County Donegal Railway conjures up! In fact, the full title of the group of lines was the County Donegal Railways Joint Committee (CDRJC). Two major railways shared its ownership, the GNR and UTA. At Strabane in Northern Ireland the CDRJC connected with the GNR's Londonderry main line whose station was alongside. It also linked end-on with the UTA's former NCC 3ft gauge line from Londonderry Victoria Road station. This line ran on the east side of the River Foyle (the competing GNR route was on the west side). From the outset the Londonderry section was worked by the CDRJC, but it had closed only a year and a half before the author's first Irish visit in 1956.

The CDRJC main line passed out of Northern Ireland just after leaving Strabane, and continued through fairly flat farmland along the track-bed of the formerly 5ft 3in gauge Finn Valley Railway. At Stranorlar the visitor could see the CDRJC's depot and workshops where its fleet of 4-6-4Ts and 2-6-4Ts was maintained. These powerful locomotives included the first Irish 3ft gauge engines to be superheated.

West of Stranorlar the railway climbed to cross the Donegal hills through the Barnesmore Gap, an effort which required the steam locomotives to be seriously extended. Donegal was a two-platform station. The track from the west end of the station led to the branch for Killybegs, a small fishing port. There was also a trailing connection east of the station from the Ballyshannon branch.

Most passenger trains were

Opposite: *The CDRJC main line between Strabane and Stranorlar had a wide formation as befits its former state as the 5ft 3in gauge Finn Valley Railway. 4-6-4T No. 11 Erne takes the morning freight away from Stranorlar on a sunny day in May 1956. The use of red-and-cream bogie brake vans made a colourful conclusion to CDR freight trains.* (Photo: Colour-Rail)

Above: *During a journey from Killybegs to Strabane on 20th July 1957, railcar No. 20 waits patiently at Castlefin on the Finn Valley section for 2-6-4T No. 6 Columbkille to pass in the loop with a westbound freight train.*

Left: *On the glorious summer evening of 19th July 1957, railcar No. 15 approaches Ballyshannon from Donegal. What a lovely bracketed signal gantry!*

Top Left: *The oldest diesel railcar to survive to the last years of the County Donegal Railways was No. 10, which was formerly No. 7 of the Clogher Valley Railway. This was a typical product of the Wigan-based company of Walker Bros., who supplied many Irish railways with articulated railcars. The power bogie carried the driving cab and the Gardner diesel engine and gearbox. The power bogie wheels were coupled with side rods which jangled as the car ran along the rails. The passenger saloon was bus-like inside, and was articulated to the back of the power bogie. No. 10 was photographed on 1st August 1956 at Stranorlar after arrival on an early morning working from Strabane.*

Bottom Left: *This busy scene shows Donegal station looking east on 20th July 1957. On the right is railcar No. 20 heading a bogie coach and a van on the 7.25am from Strabane to Killybegs. The other train in the station is the 7.45am from Killybegs to Strabane formed of railcars No. 12 and 18 with one van. 2-6-4T No. 6* Columbkille *is making up a freight train in the background. There is plenty of parcels traffic on offer this day.*

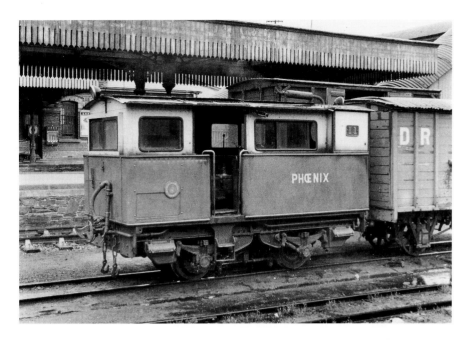

Above: *The CDR also acquired from the Clogher Valley Railway a small 0-4-0 steam tractor. The new owners rebuilt this with a railcar diesel engine and transmission, and numbered it 11 in the railcar series, naming it* Phœnix *to commemorate its metamorphosis. No. 11 was shunting at Strabane on the morning of 1st August 1956.*

worked by internal combustion engined railcars from a very early stage. The CDR had petrol engined cars from 1926 and the first diesel railcar ran in 1931. In this respect the railway was the pioneer in the British Isles for diesel traction.

The first vehicle of any kind that took the author outside the United Kingdom was CDRJC railcar No. 10. This had previously been owned by the Clogher Valley Railway, and the CDRJC had bought it when the CVR closed. Railcar 10 was a classic Gardner-Walker articulated car. Its cab was mounted on the traction bogie which also carried the engine and gearbox. The two driving axles were coupled with side rods which jangled as the railcar proceeded along the railway! To the back of

this bogie was linked the front of the passenger saloon, which in turn rode on a small bogie at the rear of the ensemble. Railcar No. 10 was of short length, and its ride was quite appalling. But it was the oldest surviving railcar on the CDRJC in 1956. Another relic of the CVR was No. 11 Phœnix. No. 11 had formerly been a 3ft gauge steam tractor. On its acquisition by the CDRJC its boiler and steam engine were removed, and were replaced by a railcar diesel engine and gearbox. This small, four-wheeled locomotive was used as the shunting engine at Stranorlar, and also worked short freights along the Finn Valley section following which it would shunt at Strabane.

The CDRJC obtained other, longer diesel railcars over the years to as late as 1951 when Nos. 19 and 20 were delivered. They attained a much higher degree of comfort than the earliest vehicles, and had more

powerful engines, up to 96hp. This enabled them to haul trailer carriages and freight vans.

Back in Strabane, the visitor could take a CDRJC train over the Strabane & Letterkenny line. This railway had once connected with the Londonderry & Lough Swilly Railway, a long, straggling line which the author regrets having been too young to see. The L&LSR had operated the largest 3ft gauge locomotives in the British Isles, including two 4-8-0 tender engines and some beefy 4-8-4Ts. By the time of his first visit, the author did see a bus in Londonderry with the fully-spelled-out name of the L&LSR painted on its sides, but that was all. ◆

7

From the LMS to the "no locomotive" railway - UTA

Northern Counties Committee

A main line railway line set out northbound from Belfast York Road station, climbed through the hills of County Antrim and flanked part of the spectacular Irish north coast on its way to Londonderry. This was formerly the main line of the Belfast & Northern Counties Railway (B&NCR). In 1903 the Midland Railway of England purchased the B&NCR and re-titled it the Midland Railway (Northern Counties Committee). The initials NCC became very familiar throughout the northern part of Ulster because they were painted on all locomotives and carriages, many of which were liveried in the classic Midland crimson colour. (A superb example is the Derby-style class U2 4-4-0 No. 74 Dunluce Castle that is

the centre-piece of the railway display in the Ulster Folk and Transport Museum at Cultra.)

The London, Midland & Scottish Railway continued to manage the railway through the Committee after the grouping of railways in Britain in 1923. Locomotives and carriages of strong Midland, and later LMS, appearance began to dominate these

railway routes that radiated out from Belfast to Larne, Londonderry, Cookstown and Portrush. By the time of the author's first visit to Ireland in 1956 there were few of the 4-4-0s left, and only three of the V class 0-6-0 freight engines. The bulk of main line traffic was undertaken by two complementary classes, the W class 2-6-0s and the WT 2-6-4Ts.

Left: *Former NCC locomotives all displayed several Derby features, betraying their Midland Railway or LMS ancestry. This locomotive taking water at Belfast York Road depot on 31st July 1956 is V class 0-6-0 No. 14. It has similarities to a Midland 3F, but also has features that hark back to the Belfast & Northern Counties Railway (B&NCR). The ABC of Irish Locomotives[1] showed the three locomotives of this class as having been built in 1923. Their ancient appearance suggests that in fact this may have been a rebuilding date rather than a new build date.*

out for fast running through the passing loops, for which the locomotives were equipped with automatic tablet-exchange apparatus. The author came on to the Irish scene too late to see the 3ft gauge lines that radiated out from Ballymena to Larne Harbour and also to the Antrim coast near Red Bay. Neither did he witness the Ballymoney-Ballycastle line. Both of these had been worked largely by strange two-cylinder compound 2-4-2Ts. A larger 2-4-4T was usually employed on the narrow gauge corridor boat express on the Ballymena to Larne line.

The author did enjoy a couple of footplate rides on the Londonderry main line, however, and he can testify to the excellent performances of which the 5ft 3in gauge 2-6-0s were capable.

Belfast & County Down Railway

The author was also too late to witness steam operation on the Belfast & County Down Railway (B&CDR). The NCC had become part of British Railways in 1948, but in 1949 had been combined with the B&CDR to be part of Northern Ireland's unified transport group, the Ulster Transport Authority. The

These locomotives had been derived from the LMS Fowler 2-6-4T design but with 6ft coupled wheels. The 2-6-4Ts had extended frames with a longer bunker, under which was an additional water tank. Both classes were superb runners and well capable of speeds up in the mid-70s (mph) when working the characteristic eight-coach formations

on the Derry and Portrush routes. They were also good hill-climbers, essential in view of the long climb over the Greenhill viaducts and beyond at 1 in 76 to a point nine miles from Belfast before the downhill run to Antrim.

This main line was double track from Belfast as far as Ballymena. Beyond there it was single track, laid

Above: *Former B&NCR and NCC principal stations were substantial structures. This is Coleraine on 20th July 1957 as class W 2-6-0 No. 93 The Foyle gallops in with the eight coaches of the 5.25pm from Belfast York Road to Portrush. This engine is one with a narrow Midland Railway design tender. Others had a wider, more modern, LMS type. Most of the class were named after northern Irish rivers. They were very lively performers, good for hill climbing as well as for high speed running on the long downhill sections.*

Below: *Following on from the W class 2-6-0 deliveries between 1933 and 1942, the NCC purchased from Derby the WT class 2-6-4Ts in two batches from 1946 to 1951. The two classes were constructed in Derby and finally assembled in Belfast York Road works. Both types were based on the LMS Fowler 2-6-4T design but with 6ft coupled wheels. Nicknamed "Jeeps", the 2-6-4Ts had reduced front valances, similar to the LMS Fairburn engines, and longer frames to accommodate an extended bunker with an extra water tank below..*

Right: *By the time of the author's first Irish visit the B&CDR had been fully dieselised. One steam locomotive remained for preservation, 4-4-2T No. 30. Typical of the group of simple suburban engines delivered by Beyer Peacock over the years between 1901 and 1921, No. 30 is seen on 31st July 1956 being restored in Belfast York Road works. This locomotive is now in the Ulster Folk and Transport Museum at Cultra.*

UTA had wasted no time in beginning the modernisation of the railway, at the same time pruning out the least economic secondary lines. The closures included all the narrow gauge sections, and all the main and branch lines of the B&CDR except the Bangor branch.

Diesels, mechanical and hydraulic

Apart from a small number of odd diesel railcars, and an even odder selection of diesel shunting locomotive prototypes from Harland & Wolff, the UTA had inherited fully steam operated railways. Modernisation therefore included the purchase of a group of suburban diesel railcars, known as the multi-engined diesels, or MEDs. These were advanced for their time, being delivered in 1953 as three-car sets with sliding door access for passengers. Each power car had two Leyland underfloor engines mounted vertically on outriggers driving through Twin-Disc hydraulic transmission units. These were subsequently replaced by epicyclic gearboxes. The UTA soon found a way of extending the operations of these successful trains. They fitted a number of NCC non-corridor coaches with through control wiring, and operated the B&CDR route with four-or six-car

sets with two or three trailer cars respectively. The surplus power cars were moved to enable dieselisation of the Larne branch; by 1957 they were operating as four-car sets with two ex-steam trailer coaches between the two power cars.

The quest continued for the elimination of steam traction. UTA gave up most freight traffic, other than containers and minor movements generally in connection with railway requirements. This enabled the UTA to develop a total-railcar policy. The next railcars to be produced were the multi-purpose diesel railcars (MPDs). UTA intended these to speed up the services to Londonderry by dint of a top speed of 90mph and more powerful engines. Each railcar was powered by one 275hp underfloor engine mounted horizontally and driving through an hydraulic torque converter. The railcars were marshalled in utterly variable formations, not as fixed sets, but

with as many railcars and trailer coaches as were needed for whatever service train they worked. Thus a Derry express could have three railcars together at one end, with others coupled outside a couple of trailer cars which might include a former steam-hauled buffet car. It was not unusual for a parcels van to bring up the rear.

They were called "multi-purpose" because two railcars in multiple were regarded as being the equivalent of a small locomotive, and were sometimes used thus to haul a few freight or container wagons, usually at night. A small group of conversions of NCC locomotive-hauled suburban stock into MPD railcars enabled additional local services out of York Road to be dieselised.

Liveries

In its earlier years UTA painted its locomotives black, and lined them out in cream and red. Such freight

Above: *A train of 1953-supplied multi-engined diesel railcars (MEDs) approaches Belfast Queen's Quay terminus on 31st July 1956, passing the former B&CDR depot and works. These dark green-and-cream liveried vehicles had been reformed by 1956 to include fewer power cars and more trailers by using former NCC suburban steam hauled coaches, thus introducing the odd slam door vehicle into rakes of sliding door stock as seen here. In the background, the main line signal (seen above the train) for the Downpatrick and Newcastle routes bears a cross sign to indicate the recent main line closure. Only the Bangor branch remained, as it does today.*

Top Right: *To speed up the services to Portrush and Londonderry, UTA introduced the multi-purpose diesels (MPDs). At Londonderry Waterside station on 26th June 1963, three MPDs head five vans on a stopping train to Belfast. These cars were liveried in a drab, plain green.*

locomotives as survived into UTA ownership, including a couple of ex-LMS 3F 0-6-0Ts, were also fully lined out. The carriages were a particularly dull, drab green. MEDs for a time had the green relieved by white upper panels, but the MPDs were unrelieved, plain dark green for many years until repainted maroon and white in the mid-1960s.

Diesel electrics
The need finally to eliminate the last steam locomotives led to the introduction in 1966 of the first diesel electric main line railcars in Northern Ireland. UTA purchased

these as underframes, bogies, power units and traction motors and control equipment from English Electric, and assembled them with new carriage bodies at Belfast Duncrue Street workshops. The power units were the EE 4SRKT type, used successfully on the British Railways Hastings, Hampshire and Oxted units. UTA refurbished and wired former NCC main line steam hauled coaches to run with these power cars. They initially operated as six-car or five-car sets, sometimes trailing a parcels van. In their maroon and white colours, the "new" trains looked smart, though

their rather drab, austere interiors soon dated. They ran the Londonderry and Portrush express trains in the fastest timings ever to be regularly achieved.

Somersaults, etc.
While much of the former NCC main line was signalled with colour light signals, many of the beautiful B&NCR somersault signals remained in use. Indeed, two pockets of these relics survive at the time of writing in mid-1997, at Castlerock on the Belfast-Londonderry main line, and on the Portrush branch. ◆

Above: *New diesel electric trains were introduced on the Belfast-Londonderry route in 1966. On 18th October 1967 the 8.35am from Belfast York Road to Londonderry threads the tunnels west of Castlerock on the spectacular stretch of railway along the north coast. The train is formed of two diesel electric power cars with four trailers between them. The trailer cars had been rebuilt at Belfast Duncrue Street carriage works from former NCC express carriages.*

8

The shortest Irish international railway - the SL&NCR

The little railway with the longest name" was the description used by Dr. E.M. Patterson in an article he had written that appeared in a railway magazine in 1956. The Sligo, Leitrim & Northern Counties Railway described the aspirations of a 5ft 3in gauge line that linked Enniskillen in Northern Ireland with the port of Sligo in the republic.

The SL&NCR lived off the agricultural trade, particularly the transport of cattle from the farms of the Counties Sligo and Leitrim to the markets in Enniskillen, and beyond via the GNR. To this effect there were in its latter years two goods trains each way each day. Each covered the 44 miles from end to end in anything up to and even beyond four hours. The fastest was undoubtedly the 7.20pm mixed from Enniskillen, which conveyed generally a string of empty cattle trucks behind its tri-composite brake coach.

Faster still (if that is the right word) were the three or so passenger trains each way that the railcars worked. The brunt of the service was covered by railcar B, the 5ft 3in gauge ultimate development of the Gardner-Walker theme. Railcar B was a smart, two-tone-green machine, articulated like the Walker cars on other railways, with coupling rods, yes, but with a driving cab at the back of the saloon, so that it could be driven from east to west without being turned. This vehicle worked a double return trip each day.

One train a day each way was worked by a railbus, one of two converted road buses like those on the GNR. Each pulled a small "hen-house-on-wheels" to convey luggage.

The goods and mixed trains were hauled by 0-6-4Ts. Beyer Peacock

had supplied all these to the SL&NCR at widely-spaced dates from 1882 to 1951. The nineteenth century 'Leitrim' class were a delight to behold with their tall chimneys and flared dome covers. The middle batch of twentieth-century engines were larger, with

Above: *This view of Manorhamilton station on 22nd July 1957 is such a peaceful and old-world scene that it is difficult to grasp that the locomotive is the last steam locomotive to be delivered new to the railways of Ireland! The Beyer Peacock 0-6-4T Lough Erne, together with its sister engine Lough Melvin, was received by the SL&NCR as recently as 1951. These two locomotives were the line's most powerful, and enabled the earliest 0-6-4Ts of the 1882 "Leitrim" class to be scrapped.*

Above: *The veteran 0-6-4T Hazlewood was the last of the "Leitrim" class, the original Beyer Peacock engines built for the SL&NCR from 1882 to 1890. Hazlewood was in Manorhamilton depot when seen on 22nd July 1957. The SL&NCR was constructed to light railway principles; thus the locomotives carried re-railing jacks and had additional coupling chains on their buffer beams.*

Left: *The SL&NCR ran the last steam hauled real mixed train in the British Isles, the 7.20pm from Enniskillen to Sligo. On 1st August 1956 the good Sir Henry (Beyer Peacock 1904) stands with the mixed for customs examination at Belcoo. On this day, Sir Henry leads coach No. 9 plus seven empty cattle wagons and a goods brake van. This was a one-way passenger working, the coach being brought back to Enniskillen each day in the consist of the morning freight from Sligo. Note the light section, flat-bottomed rail used on this cheaply constructed line.*

bigger boilers and cylinders. The two engines of the final batch had sat on the quay-side at Birkenhead while the manufacturers attempted to get payment out of the impecunious railway. Failing this, they attached cast nameplates on the bunkers stating that Beyer Peacock owned the locomotives, and dispatched them under a lease arrangement in 1951.

Beyer Peacock were present when the assets of the railway, which had closed in 1957, were put up for auction. They succeeded in selling their two machines to the UTA who later used them as Belfast area shunters. One has been preserved. The rest of the SL&NCR rolling stock assets went for scrap, apart from railcar B which CIÉ bought, numbered 2509, and ran for a few seasons between Limerick and Nenagh. ◆

Above: *Railbuses and this railcar worked all but one of the SL&NCR passenger services each day. Railcar B is seen arriving at Enniskillen on the 4.40pm service from Sligo on 1st August 1956. This vehicle is a development of the Gardner-Walker railcar type used on the CDRJC and GNR, and was duo-directional. The foreground tracks belonged to the GNR route from Clones.*

Below: *Coach No. 9 was a permanent feature of the 7.20pm mixed from Enniskillen to Sligo. The carriage was a tri-composite brake vehicle, arguably the last clerestory coach built for any railway in the British Isles. Its appearance on 1st August 1956 suggests that it had never been repainted since it was new in the mid-1920s.*

9

The Great Northern divided

Someone once described the Great Northern Railway of Ireland as the last example of co-operation between the Northern Ireland and Éireann governments. While this is an extreme and inaccurate view, what happened to the GNR in and after 1958 illustrates the concept perfectly.

Nearly bankrupt

Received wisdom states that in September 1958 the board of the GNR declared to the two governments that its financial position was such that it would have to cease treading within two weeks. Government money was quickly made available to stave off that frightening action, but clearly something had to be done. The GNR had been nationalised by both

Left: *Until the GNR was dismembered in 1958 one never saw former NCC locomotives anywhere near CIÉ coaching stock. The break-up of the railway between the two countries gave rise to the inefficient practice of changing locomotives at the border on the Belfast-Dublin main line. At the same time, surplus W and WT class engines from the former NCC section of UTA were drafted to the GN section. Thus, on 25th June 1963, class WT 2-6-4T No. 54 had taken over the 9.15am from Dublin at Dundalk and was facing the climb over the border hills with a light green CIÉ coach next to the engine. The train had arrived at Dundalk behind two CIÉ GM Bo-Bo diesels.*

Right: *The split-up of the GNR meant that CIÉ diesel locomotives Nos. B154 and B144 hauling the 9.15am from Dublin to Belfast on 25th June 1963 would be replaced by a UTA steam locomotive when they reached Dundalk. The train was photographed arriving at Drogheda; the leading three vehicles were former GNR coaches in CIÉ green, and were removed at Dundalk in view of the reduced amount of traffic crossing the border in the mid-1960s*

countries in 1953 when they had appointed the Great Northern Railway Board to run it. Public ownership was already the principal way of running major public service enterprises in Eire, and was also the norm in the U.K. at the time. In 1958 the two governments decided to dismember the GNR and split it between the two countries, north and south of the border.

Split

All railway lines and infrastructure north of the border were handed to the UTA. All those south of the border went to CIÉ. There was geographic logic to that. How the traction and rolling stock was divided between the two concerns

evoked much more surprise. One suspects a speedy, unthinking political hand (or hands) in deciding that the fleet should be split exactly evenly between the two railways. This had the illogical effect of dividing every class of locomotive as evenly as possible between UTA and CIÉ, irrespective of which depots the locomotives were previously allocated to, or where they worked, or whether the traffic was really identical on each side of the border. The graceful compounds were divided in a 2:3 split, and the VSs in a 3:2 split.

Top Right: *A strange quirk of the division of GNR motive power between CIÉ and UTA was the need in the early 1960s for the railways to trade steam locomotives. Class S 4-4-0 No. 171 Slieve Gullion had been sold by CIÉ to UTA by the time it was seen being turned at Portadown depot on 25th June 1963. 171 had retained its GNR blue livery and its number, only the "CIÉ" stencil on the buffer beam giving away its recent ownership.*

Bottom Right: *UTA painted most of its GNR locomotive acquisitions in a smart lined black livery, though it was a shadow of the former glory of the GNR blue. Carrying the number 62, the former No. 190 Lugnaquilla stands alongside the roof-damaged shed at Londonderry Foyle Road depot on 26th June 1963.*

Left: *The only steam locomotive working in the republic that the author and his friend saw during their 1963 visit was former NCC class W 2-6-0 No. 91 The Bush! This had arrived with a Sunday return excursion from Belfast on 22nd June 1963. It was photographed at Dublin Amiens Street during the layover before the excursion returned north. (This was one of the locomotives that had large, LMS style tenders.)*

The sensible opportunity, for example, of sending the five VS class engines to Belfast Adelaide depot and the five compounds to Dublin Amiens Street was passed by.

Numbering

CIÉ quickly stencilled its initials on the buffer beams of steam locomotives, and marked a letter 'N' against the cabside number to identify them apart from its own locomotives. No repainting was carried out, because CIÉ was already on the way to eliminating steam traction and intended to dispose of the GNR fleet at the earliest opportunity.

UTA on the other hand

Below: *Class WT 2-6-4T No. 55 approaches Dundalk with a Belfast-Dublin express on 25th June 1963. Here it was replaced by a pair of GM Co-Cos for the run to Dublin. The carriages are former GNR stock repainted by the two railways in various shades of green.*

assimilated those GNR locomotives for which it could see further need into its own numbering scheme, and repainted and branded them all in standard UTA lined black, other than the V and VS 4-4-0s which remained blue. Thus the UTA improved the freight 0-6-0s visually by lining them out, but most of the blue 4-4-0s lost their bright colours. Any GNR engine for which UTA could not foresee extended use was stencilled "UTA" and given a letter 'X' below its cab-side number. In the event, some of these lasted five or more years!

Mixed stock

Soon the observer could see GNR coaching stock operating on the Belfast-Dublin main line in both UTA dark green, and CIÉ black-and-gold, sometimes in the same train. Standard CIÉ coaches on Commonwealth bogies, often in light green livery, also appeared, extending the variety.

Closures

UTA led the way in decimating the cross-border routes. From 1959 onwards, lines that penetrated the border regions were summarily cut out by UTA, leaving CIÉ with several disconnected rumps on the Éireann side. This forced CIÉ to initiate many closures, too, a little less willingly perhaps, but in practice unavoidable. Thus the Belfast-Dublin line became the only railway to cross Ireland's border, and the only ex-GNR route to remain in Eire.

Changing engines

A real operating nonsense started after the GNR was dismembered, in the new practice of changing engines on through trains at the border station of Dundalk. CIÉ began to introduce diesel locomotives on the route in the early 1960s, but was initially unwilling to let them run into Northern Ireland. By then UTA's multi-purpose diesel railcars

Above: *The one visible benefit from the GNR split on the motive power front was that the GNR freight locomotives that were received by the UTA were painted in lined out black livery instead of plain black. UTA No. 47 was a former GNR class UG 0-6-0, its high-sided tender suggesting that it was one of the 1948 batch. It is seen arriving at Dungannon with a stopping train from Omagh on 26th June 1963.*

had rendered many W 2-6-0s and WT 2-6-4Ts surplus to requirements, so these were drafted to the Belfast-Dundalk section to work the express services. A few excursion trains from Belfast to the Irish capital did use W or WT locomotives throughout, but these were the exceptions. (For this extended duty, some of the WTs ran with tenders attached for additional water supply.) The delay caused by changing engines at Dundalk in the

middle of what was once a relatively fast 113 mile journey did nothing to encourage passenger traffic.

Locomotives for sale

In 1963, the imbalance of ex-GNR locomotives between UTA and CIÉ provided an opportunity for further change. CIÉ had by then ceased to use GNR (or almost any other) steam traction, but UTA wanted to avoid repairs to the locomotives it had. Viable locomotives were available in the south, so CIÉ sold some to UTA. Among these, S class 4-4-0 No. 171 *Slieve Gullion*, still in blue and lettered "CIE" on its front buffer beam, worked between Belfast and Portadown for a time. At least one VS 4-4-0, No. 207 *Boyne*, also moved north for UTA suburban work. Neither was repainted, nor renumbered into UTA stock.

Through running

By the time of the author's 1967 visit, the two railways had managed to co-operate to the extent that through running was once again the norm, but the traffic on offer had sunk to the minimum seen on the route. (This was actually before the resumption of significant terrorism that began in 1968.) Four 'Enterprise' trains each way each day sufficed for the through traffic. The train set supplied by UTA was a four-car ex-GNR diesel railcar set, now in maroon and white livery. CIÉ sent a GM Bo-Bo diesel locomotive with four Cravens coaches on B.5 bogies (see Chapter 11). Thus the capacity provided on Ireland's capital main line was almost a quarter what it had been in GNR times. ◆

10

Guinness genius

Small 1ft 10in gauge steam locomotives used to operate in the heart of Dublin on a railway system that included a spiral tunnel of two and a half turns graded at 1 in 40. And these little engines could operate on the 5ft 3in gauge as well!

The Irish genius whose engineering vision gave birth to the compact 0-4-0Ts on the 1ft 10in gauge system at St. James's Gate brewery was Samuel Geoghegan. He was faced by the challenge to link three of the levels of the brewery by a transport system that could carry sacks of hops and malt, and barrels of the finished porter more effectively than could horses and carts.

The major restraint on locomotive design was the height and width of the tunnel section. Mr. Geoghegan's design turned the normal steam locomotive up-side down. He provided high plate frames, one on each side of the locomotive, with the marine type boiler mounted between them. The cylinder block bridged the frames above the boiler just behind the top of the smokebox. The connecting rods turned a crankshaft over the firebox, which in turn drove vertical rods that drove the rear pair of coupled wheels. The water supply was held in side tanks that were riveted outside the side frames. The driver stood on a small rear platform that doubled as the coal bunker. A sizeable fleet of at least 19 locomotives was turned out from William Spence & Co.'s Cork

Left: *The genius that was Guinness! No. 22 illustrates Samuel Geoghegan's brilliant concept of a very small narrow gauge steam locomotive suitable for working in the Dublin brewery's spiral tunnel. The design was based on a combination of railway, traction engine and marine technology. The cylinder block bridged the main frames above the boiler and drove a crankshaft located over the firebox. Vertical rods connected with the pins on the fly cranks of the rear coupled wheels. There was even room for a long chimney giving a decent draught to the fire! No. 22 was seen on standby duty outside the depot in St. James's Gate brewery on 3rd August 1956.*

Street Foundry in Dublin in the early 1910s, and these worked the system right through until the 1950s.

At the loading bay area near the River Liffey there were 5ft 3in gauge sidings on which railway wagons were placed for unloading and loading. A tramway link across and along the streets to Kingsbridge station goods yard enabled the finished Guinness barrels to be transported to their Irish customers. Two Hudswell Clarke 0-4-0STs, Nos. 2 and 3, shunted these sidings. It seems that the company worked all its broad gauge locomotives on a planned 100% availability roster. Rather than buy a spare broad gauge engine, Samuel Geoghegan had the idea to use one or two of the smaller and cheaper 1ft 10in gauge locomotives as standby to the broad gauge machines. His genius emerged yet again!

Nowhere else, to the author's knowledge has he seen anything like the haulage wagon system devised by Samuel Geoghegan. It really was so simple, that genius is the only word to describe it. The author saw three such wagons at the St. James's Gate site during his visit in 1956, all

derrick into this space, its 1ft 10in gauge wheels rested on four flangeless wheels within the wagon. The flangeless wheels were linked through reduction gearing to the broad gauge wheels of the wagon. There was no need for brackets, bolts, jacks, clamps or screws, the conventional methods that the average British engineer would use to attach a prime mover to the inside of a propulsion vehicle. The small engine was a neat fit inside the wagon. Gravity (and some judiciously applied sand) was sufficient for internal traction, and that was that! The author's friend Mark Abbott photographed one of these combinations shunting the broad gauge sidings as late as 1957.

The transfer of broad gauge wagons between the brewery and Kingsbridge yard was usually in the charge of a Hudswell "constant horsepower" diesel locomotive, No. 4. The locomotive supervisor was

> **❝***As the visitors were being shown around the Guinness brewery in Dublin in 1956 a voice from the group asked, "Are you allowed a pint or two while you are at work?" Without batting an eyelid the gentle old guide replied, "Well, you don't work in an orchard without eating some apples!*❞

either in use or serviceable. Each wagon had outside frames and buffer beams, with the space between them shaped as a neat fit for one of the narrow gauge engines. When a small locomotive was lowered from a

Above: *Two narrow gauge locomotives sit in their haulage wagons on standby duty for the broad gauge locomotives at the Guinness brewery, Dublin, on 3rd August 1956. Was there ever a stranger sight?*

Right: *Samuel Geoghegan's genius extended to the simple haulage wagons he designed to enable the 1ft 10in gauge locomotives to work on the broad gauge lines in St. James's Gate brewery. Just drop a small locomotive into the specially shaped hole in the wagon, and the locomotive wheels are ready to drive the inner wheels of the wagon by adhesion. The 5ft 3in gauge railway wheels were driven through the large gearboxes that are visible in this overhead view.*

not enamoured by that machine, and always held at least one narrow gauge locomotive in steam in a haulage wagon in reserve.

In 1951 the author saw a tiny, blue diesel shunting locomotive on display alongside a large Indian Railways broad gauge 2-8-2 steam locomotive at the Festival of Britain exhibition on London's South Bank. This little diesel was one of the batch of four-wheeled locomotives that Guinness had ordered from F.C. Hibbert & Co. as replacements for the Geoghegan steam locomotives. Most narrow gauge traffic within St. James's Gate at the time of the author's visit was being handled by these small machines, but one steam engine was outside the depot in reserve for them. Two others were in haulage wagons backing up the broad gauge locomotives. The supervisor told the author that the diesels could not be used in haulage wagons, so keeping the steam machines was vital to the

Above: *Two Hudswell Clarke 0-4-0STs shunted the sidings at the loading sheds. They also deputised for the Hudswell 0-4-0 diesel that operated the street section for transferring wagons to and from the CIÉ yard at Kingsbridge. The only standby for the three locomotives was the haulage wagon system using the narrow gauge engines. No. 2 was photographed on 3rd August 1956.*

smooth running of the brewery.

Alongside the brewery, horses were struggling to lift cart loads of raw materials up the steep roadway

from the river to the top level of the complex. Down by the river side, men were craning barrels of the dark liquid into the steam barge *Sandyford* for their trip down the river to the docks, in the company of five men on board. It was all very labour intensive.

Nowadays, the Guinness railways are no more. Lorries bring in the raw products. Lorries trip the products of St. James's Gate to the railway yard in containers for distribution by container train, and to the docks for loading on to the container ships that shift a multiplicity of Ireland's and Europe's products all over the world. At least three of the small Geoghegan locomotives are in museums in Ireland and the U.K. So is one of the Planet diesels. ◆

Below: *The replacements for the Geoghegan steam locomotives were supposed to be the group of Hibbert Planet 0-4-0 diesel shunters that were delivered early in the 1950s. One can judge from their shape that they were intended also to fit in the haulage wagons. The supervisor at St. James's Gate whom the author and his friend met was adamant that they would not fit, and that the small number of surviving steam locomotives was essential for standby purposes.*

11

CIÉ: GMs all round

New General Motors locomotives

The low availability of the A and C class Metro Vick/ Crossley diesels in the late 1950s caused a severe shortage of traction power on CIÉ, such that the elimination of steam power was delayed. Then came dismemberment of the GNR in 1958, which added to the routes on which CIÉ locomotives had to operate. Speedy and desperate measures were needed. A first step was to buy twelve General Motors (GM) standard 950hp Bo-Bo switchers geared for 75mph operation. These arrived quickly in 1960 and were immediately successful. CIÉ discovered that at last they had a diesel locomotive type that needed less maintenance and many fewer repairs, a type that ran reliably with high availability.

So successful were these 15

Above: *The double-cab General Motors Bo-Bos have become the hall-mark of the second generation of CIÉ diesel traction. Class 141 950hp locomotive No. B175 leaves Dublin Kingsbridge terminus on 22nd June 1963 with a down express formed of mixed Inchicore and Park Royal stock. The four-wheeled heating van is unusually the second vehicle in the train.*

locomotives, the B121 class, that CIÉ decided to buy more of the type, but persuaded GM to customise them, better to match Irish conditions. Thus the 37 examples of the B141 class had conventional European cabs at each end, while retaining the narrow body profile, giving them a strange appearance to British (and Irish) eyes. The B141 class had 950hp diesel engines, but the next group to be ordered, the 12

locomotives of the B181 class, were given engines of 1,100hp.

The GM Bo-Bo fleet quickly established itself as the backbone of the CIÉ traction fleet. Pairs of locomotives worked the heavier

expresses while single units sufficed for the lighter passenger and freight trains. The A class were relegated to main line freight and secondary route passenger trains, such as those to Rosslare or Sligo, while the C class

led a twilight existence having lost most of the light duties for which they were originally designed.

Pioneering rebuilds

As a result of the positive performance results of the GM locomotives, CIÉ's chief mechanical engineer and his staff, frustrated by the unreliability and heavy costs of the A and C classes, produced their trump card. They became the first non-American railway engineers to persuade the giant General Motors company that they were capable of fitting GM engines to non-GM-designed locomotives. They experimentally fitted six A class locomotives with GM engines, still driving the sturdy Metro-Vick generators. These were so successful that the remaining 54 of the class were re-engined in 1968-

1971 at 1,325hp. Six carried even higher rated engines of 1,650hp. These tended to be used on the heavier expresses.

CIÉ had bought the feeble 550hp C class for light passenger and freight trains such as operated the many small branch lines. Most of these routes, the main *raison d'être* of the C class, had gone, but there was a need for more powerful locomotives to complement the A and B classes. CIÉ realised that the Metro-Vick electric traction equipment in the C class was extremely robust, and well able to deliver twice the power demanded by the original C class design. CIÉ re-engined all 34 of them with 1,100hp GM engines! Reclassified as class B201, they quickly established themselves as good machines for the Dublin suburban services and for short-haul main line freights. In this

guise, they became "really useful engines" for the first time and lasted until displaced by the DART electric service and by mark 3 push-pull trains in the late-1980s. Indeed, for part of their time in inner suburban service the B201 class locomotives were coupled to de-engined diesel railcars used as push-pull units. This demise of the once-comfortable d.m.u.s was regrettable. Such spartan seating was provided in the name of vandal-resistance that the vehicles did not encourage much custom.

Higher speed to Cork

Meanwhile, the need for more speed on the Cork main line led to an order for 18 large GM Co-Co locomotives of 2,450hp. These 071 class, 90mph machines were delivered in 1976. The use of type letters, A, B, C, etc.

Left: *When they were re-engined with 1,350hp General Motors engines in the mid 1960s, the Metro-Vick A class Co-Cos received a new lease of life. They became fit to handle reliably main line passenger and heavy freight duties on all but the fastest trains. With the general renumbering in the 1970s the A class became known as the 001 class and received one or two zeros in front of their previous numbers. Other locomotives merely lost their class prefixes. The temporary "S" suffix on No. 049, seen at the fuel point at Limerick on 14th May 1988, denoted that the locomotive was equipped to work with the new signalling in the Dublin suburban DART area. Note the container train of long-wheelbase four-wheeled wagons in the right background.*

Above: *From the 1970s, block freight working became the rule on CIÉ. Most were single product trains, but general merchandise was handled in container trains. Metro-Vick/GM class 001 Co-Co No. 023 passes through Kildare with the morning train of anhydrous ammonia from Marino Point on the Cobh branch to Arklow on 12th May 1988.*

Below: *The re-engining of the former C class with GM 1,100hp engines doubled their individual power output at a stroke! This enabled them to be usefully employed on medium weight freight trains and on branch and suburban passenger trains with reasonable performance. 201 class Metro-Vick/GM Bo-Bo No. 232 calls at the former MGWR platforms in Dublin Connolly station with a southbound outer suburban train on 12th May 1988. The train is formed largely of 1950s Park Royal stock.*

to describe locomotive power ranges had by then been abandoned by CIÉ. The 071s were immediately successful and operated the principal trains on all CIÉ main lines except those to Sligo and Rosslare Harbour.

Air-conditioning

A number of serious accidents with passenger trains had led the Irish government to insist that future designs of carriages should not have timber framed bodies but be built with "heavy steel underframes". CIÉ was encouraged to replace the 1960s Inchicore-built, timber framed, steel panelled coaches because of their poor performance in crash conditions. In 1972 delivery took place of new, B.R.-designed air-conditioned mark 2d stock built by Derby works and finished out at Inchicore for the principal main line services. To British eyes the brown moquette covered standard class seats with PVC headrests were a bit basic, but they were practical and reasonably comfortable, and a great improvement on the older stock which they replaced. All timber bodied stock and many of the popular Park Royal vehicles disappeared at this time, with more being broken up when the mark 3s arrived in 1984.

These B.R.-style mark 3 coaches were the first locomotive hauled trains in Ireland to have power-operated swing plug doors. There was no precedent for this in the U.K. at the time, and CIÉ engineers had a major task in getting the doors to work reliably. Nonetheless, by persistence they did make them work. The carriage interiors were excellent, with deep pile carpeting in standard class (there is nowadays very little first class in Ireland) and well padded, moquette-trimmed seats. The early mark 3s were built complete in Derby, but later ones came over as skeletons to be fitted out in Dublin. The last 24 of the 124 did not enter InterCity service, but were built from scratch at Inchicore as outer suburban push-pull trains.

Below: *Container traffic in Ireland operates generally on bogie flat wagons, though originally many four-wheeled wagons were converted for the service. 1,100hp Bo-Bo No. 192 of class 181 passes through Drogheda with a container train for Northern Ireland on 19th October 1992. The containers will be off-loaded at Belfast Adelaide yard, on the site of the former GNR steam locomotive depot.*

Above: *New mark 3 outer suburban trains were supplied by Inchicore works in 1989. Some single-cab 121 class were re-engined with 1,100hp engines from withdrawn 201 class locomotives. The hopper windows in the coach bodysides are clearly visible in this view of No. 128 arriving at Drogheda with the 11.24 from Dublin Pearse on 19th October 1992.*

Outer suburban

The typical Dublin outer suburban train that ran to Drogheda or Dundalk was a short train of Park Royal or Cravens vehicles headed by a GM double-cab Bo-Bo with a heating van. Running round at each end of the trip was time and resource consuming. CIÉ's engineers took the chance to modify the design of the last 24 of the mark 3 coaches. The requirement was for pressure-ventilation, so they removed the cooling equipment from the air-conditioning modules, and fitted new hopper windows to the body sides in alternate positions to provide some ventilation. This altered the external appearance of the coaches significantly. An excellent and handsome design of front end for the driving trailers was developed via a mock-up built at Inchicore.

Locomotives for the push-pull trains were taken from the single-cab 121 class. The single cabs had always been seen as a restraint on the locomotives' flexibility, and the chance to use them where one cab was enough was sensible. However, six mark 3 coaches is a mite heavy for a 950hp Bo-Bo to shift at a useful speed (shadows of the C class again?), so the push-pull 121s were re-engined with 1,100hp GM units taken from redundant class B201 locomotives. The introduction of these trains proved popular, though their running times were necessarily unadventurous.

The oldest coaches running on CIÉ lines at this time were the Park Royals, most of which dated from the early 1950s. Their demise had to wait until the next era of Irish dieselisation.

Freight

CIÉ was among the first railways in the world consciously to get out of wagonload freight. It recognised that the activity of shunting wagons at marshalling yards is extremely costly. Remarshalling trains that are en route is even more so, as well as being a source of extended transit times. CIÉ rearranged all its freight

Above: *The push-pull driving trailer No. 6102, seen at Drogheda on 19th October 1992, shows the placement under the middle of the vehicle of the auxiliary diesel alternator set. The alternator provides power for train heat, light and control. The coaches have basic suburban style seating, pressure ventilation and power operated swing plug doors.*

Below: *The eighteen 2,450hp GM Co-Cos were the front line express train power until the advent of the new 201 class in 1994. Class 071 Co-Co No. 071 runs round its train of mark 3 InterCity coaches at Cork Kent station on 11th May 1988 in readiness to forming the 14.45 to Dublin Heuston.*

into end-to-end block workings. Less-than-trainload traffic was catered for by running container trains. Other trains were basically single-product trains geared to the country's economy, mainly minerals, fertilisers and chemicals.

Any shunting that remained was placed under the responsibility of the train engine so it proved possible for CIÉ to withdraw all its diesel shunting locomotives. Only at Heuston and Connolly stations, Dublin, are GM Bo-Bos used regularly as station pilot locomotives, actually performing the duty for which the original American type was designed!

Stations

Politics influences much of Ireland's development, even railways. A move to rename the principal stations in Dublin and other cities led to people having to learn new names for familiar places. Kingsbridge became Heuston station; Amiens Street was renamed Connolly; and Westland Row is now Pearse. Cork Glanmire Road became Cork Kent station. Readers with a basic knowledge of modern Irish history will understand the patriotic nature of the names used. Even now, the old names sometimes surface in conversation. ◆

Above: *Grand old edifices persist in forming contrasts with the new diesel age! Dominated by the signal cabin on its bridge spanning the tracks at the west end of Waterford station, class 071 Co-Co No. 079 awaits departure with the 10.50 to Dublin Heuston on 12th May 1988.*

12

DART - Dublin's electrics

When enthusiasts visited Dublin in the late 1950s it surely never occurred to most of them that there was anything amiss with the suburban train pattern. It seemed quite natural that the GNR should run diesel units to Howth, and that CIÉ should drag trainloads of commuters to Bray and beyond behind ancient, wheezing steam locomotives, or in smart new diesel railcars. Certainly, the idea that trains might one day run throughout between Howth and Bray was not on the agenda.

Indeed, as has been hinted in the previous chapter, CIÉ made little effort to make suburban travel comfortable, being more interested at the time in reducing costs to counteract the revenue drop from a reducing clientele.

Therefore the vision that CIÉ conceived of an electrified railway from Howth through Dublin to Bray

Right: *The advent of the DART electric trains around Dublin Bay from Bray in the south to Howth on its peninsular revolutionised Dubliners' attitudes towards railways and rail travel. The smart, two-tone green, 1,500V dc electric multiple unit sets have proved to be extremely popular, and provide a frequent regular service throughout the day. Two trains pass in Blackrock station on 1st September 1984.*

was a bold one. With overhead wires pressed at 1,500V dc, the new trains that entered service in 1984 were a delight to behold, both inside and out. Externally they looked very smart in a two-tone green livery not too dissimilar to that borne many years before by the SL&NCR railcar B! Thirteen years later, as this chapter is written, the DART trains' paintwork is still surviving, though close examination shows its age. The original finish by the carriage manufacturers, Linke Hoffmann Busch of Germany, was superb. The reliable traction equipment had been made in England by GEC and shipped to Germany for assembly in the trains.

Internally the trains are wide and airy. Clean, quite comfortable low-backed bench seats, are arranged two-plus-two each side of the aisle, being trimmed in a smart green moquette. The DART branding - Dublin Area Rapid Transit - has its distinctive badge and colouring. This colouring is even carried over on to the walls of the depot at Fairview, north of Connolly station. Fairview depot maintains the DART trains with economical staffing levels, and with good reliability.

The DART railway is the pride of Ireland: the little two-car sets normally run in pairs, and trains are rarely more than 15 minutes apart. During the peaks they are more frequent. The author has seen them many times in films and on television, as the DART train is an "in" place for Irish celebrities to be filmed and interviewed. No wonder that the rush hours see these trains packed, and running at high frequencies of which the former GNR and GSR would never have dreamed.

Along with the trains, the stations on the DART route were upgraded, all part of the aim to brighten up the travel experience. Signalling has been modernised. The DART e.m.u.s are subject to a form of automatic train control from track-based beacons that control their approach speeds and take over the

Top Right: *A train of two two-car DART units leaves Dublin Pearse station southbound for Bray on 13th May 1988. As the sun shines on the paint-work, the observer can see the success with which the two shades of green link modernity with the proper colour for the "emerald isle".*

Bottom Right: *In the first year of electric operation of the Dublin suburban services, two e.m.u. sets stand at Bray station on 31st August 1984 in readiness for departure for Dublin and Howth. In the south bay in the background stands a Metro-Vick/GM class 201 Bo-Bo with the push-pull shuttle for Greystones that operated until replaced by a road bus a few years later. Its two coaches are former diesel multiple unit cars shorn of their traction equipment and fitted with spartan suburban seating.*

braking if the driver does not react to signals and speed restrictions. Such is the modernity of a railway that not too long before had almost been written off as of no value. The DART's contribution to alleviating Dublin's chronic traffic congestion is highly significant. ◆

Below: *Two two-car sets approach Blackrock en route to Bray on 1st September 1984. The Howth peninsular is visible in the background.*

13

NIR is born - and locomotives come back to the north

The term "Northern Ireland Railways" began as a marketing term by UTA in 1967. When the author stayed overnight at a fine hotel in Castlerock, just near the station, he noticed that the railway promotional material was lettered "NIR". He also saw that some of the maroon and white stock of the new diesel electric Londonderry trains had NIR branding on the carriage sides. In 1968, however, the separate, wholly owned company of NIR was born, as a result of UTA's restructuring. The NIR company survived as a nationally owned entity in its own right until being merged with Ulsterbus in 1995.

New 'Enterprise'

Following the successful replacement of the Derry trains, NIR turned its attention to its share of the Belfast-Dublin main line expresses. The old GNR diesel mechanical units looked good in maroon and white, but the gloss belied their general mechanical deterioration. In addition, the railway was confronting increasing traffic. In 1970 a new 'Enterprise' set was introduced. In formation, this was a unique train in the history of U.K. railways at that time. Three new Bo-Bo diesel electric locomotives were supplied by Hunslet, who had sub-contracted their assembly to the British Rail BREL works at Doncaster. These locomotives contained eight-cylinder 1,350hp English Electric power units driving generators that included train heat windings. In action they sounded like British Rail class 20s.

Above: *Northern Ireland Railways put an end to the all-railcar policy of their parent UTA with the purchase of the three Hunslet/BREL class 101 Bo-Bo diesel electrics for the 'Enterprise' service. On 16th May 1988 the photographer at Belfast Adelaide was very lucky indeed to be able to photograph Nos. 102 (leading) and 101 topping and tailing the 09.00 from Belfast Central to Dublin Connolly. On this morning the normal GM-hauled train set had been withdrawn for special cleaning and preparation for the after-noon publicity launch of a new through service from Belfast to Dun Laoghaire. The two Hunslets and a rake of five mark 2abcs had been substituted for it. The extended working to Dun Laoghaire turned out to be a short-lived initiative.*

Right: *NIR inherited a fleet of diesel mechanical railcars from the GNR section of UTA and also the diesel hydraulics and diesel electrics from the NCC section. It took some years to rationalise these to a more-or-less common type. A former GNR four-car set, now in maroon-and-white livery, threads the curves near Poyntzpass on the climb to the summit of the line with the 14.30 'Enterprise' from Belfast to Dublin on 17th October 1967.*

They were the only locomotives in Ireland to provide electric train heat until the advent of new locomotives in the republic in 1994.

BREL also delivered a small fleet of new carriages to the then current BR mark 2 pressure-ventilated design. The 'Enterprise' train set was designed to operate as an eight coach formation at times of heavy traffic. A Hunslet Bo-Bo at each end of the train provided enough power to maintain timings. When traffic was lighter, a reduced formation of five coaches was employed. This needed only one of the locomotives, the train being operated push-pull using a mark 2 driving trailer. The locomotives carried a smart mid-blue livery, but the coaches received a strange mixture of maroon upper panels and royal blue below the windows.

New multiple units

This maroon-and-blue livery was also a hall-mark of the class 80 diesel electric multiple units that were ordered from BREL to replace the remaining GNR- and UTA-inspired railcars. The class 80 units were based on the BR mark 2 carriage design. Each power car carried an English Electric 4SRKT 550hp diesel engine. The power car bodies were mounted on second-hand BR mark 1 underframes riding on mark 6 motor bogies only one of which was motored. The trailer cars were to the standard integral body mark 2 design, on B.5 bogies. These thoroughly competent and useful units have been, since their introduction, the mainstay of Northern Ireland's internal train services.

New link

Until the 1970s the three sections of NIR still operated as disconnected, separate railways. The Bangor

branch had its Belfast terminus at Queen's Quay. Trains from Londonderry and Larne came into the York Road terminus in the north of the city. Trains from Dublin and Portadown arrived at the former GNR terminus in Great Victoria Street, near the central bus station.

NIR built a brand new station on the double track freight-only Belfast union line that connected the former GNR and B&CDR systems. Belfast Central was modern in

appearance, though of somewhat austere and morose aspect as befitted an economy that was under constant threat from terrorist action. Consequently, the Central station was surrounded by enormous wire fences, and passengers could be subjected to frisking by security staff on entry to the station premises. Nonetheless, the opening of Belfast Central enabled Great Victoria Street and Queen's Quay stations to be closed.

Above: *Under its two masters, the Dublin-Belfast main line received very little investment for many years. GNR style, lower quadrant semaphore signals, and even a locomotive watering tank and column, dominate this scene at Lisburn on 2nd September 1984. The re-routing of the Belfast to Londonderry trains via the former GNR freight line from Lisburn to Antrim via Crumlin enabled Derry trains better to connect at Lisburn and at Belfast Central with other services. Class 80 d.e.m.u. power car No. 83 enters Lisburn with a Belfast to Londonderry train. The unit is liveried in maroon and dark blue. New multiple aspect signals were commissioned on the main line shortly afterwards. The water tank is still there in 1997.*

To make a positive connection between the Derry route and the rest of the system, NIR chose to abandon the York Road to Antrim section (other than for stock movements). Trains from Londonderry diverged from the former main line at Antrim and ran on the former GNR freight-only single track to Lisburn, reaching Belfast Central from the south west. This put some 20 minutes extra into the schedules, but gave Crumlin a service for the first time for very many years. Only the Larne line was then isolated from the rest of the NIR network. A shuttle bus was set up to link the Central and York Road stations via Belfast city centre.

Right: *New d.e.m.u.s were required to replace the old English Electric 70 class units that had relied on refurbished steam stock for their trailer cars. Two of the then new BREL-built "Castle" class three-car units for the Larne service stand at Belfast York Road on 16th May 1988. The similarity of the carriage bodies with British Rail suburban multiple units is obvious. The bodies rest on former BR mark 1 underframes with mark 6 motor bogies and B.5 trailer bogies. The power car cab ends are non-gangwayed. The electric traction equipment had been recovered from earlier NIR units.*

Above: A new livery for d.e.m.u.s that was introduced in 1984 used a background of light grey on the bodysides with a maroon band below the windows, and maroon cab fronts. On 16th May 1988, power car No. 98 propels a morning train from Belfast to Lisburn out of Adelaide station. The yard in the background occupies the site of the former GNR locomotive depot and is host to some bogie fertiliser wagons and a tank train hauled by an Irish Rail GM Bo-Bo.

Below: NIR purchased first two, then later a third, GM Co-Cos of the same design as the Irish Rail 071 class. Nos. 111 to 113 are named after three of the former railways in Northern Ireland. This view shows No. 111 Great Northern standing at Belfast Central with the 09.00 to Dublin Connolly on 1st September 1984. The livery is plain mid-blue with a strikingly large NIR symbol.

New locomotives

Despite the activities of those who would disrupt normal railway life, traffic on the international route south to Dublin kept increasing throughout the 1970s and early 1980s. An additional 'Enterprise' train was needed. NIR ordered two (and later a third) General Motors Co-Cos (class 111), identical to the

18 CIÉ ones of class 071. More mark 2s came across from Britain, second-hand examples that had been rebogied to 5ft 3in gauge. The Belfast-Dublin service now consisted of two NIR mark 2 sets and one air-conditioned one from CIÉ, each train running two return trips, giving six through trains a day in each direction each of seven to nine coaches. The NIR locomotive-hauled train sets hauled by the class 111 locomotives had their train heat supply generators in one brake coach, not as a separate vehicle as was CIÉ practice.

Meanwhile, a number of the diesel electric multiple units (d.e.m.u.s) had been sent to England for repair to bomb damage. The Hunslet locomotives were able to help out by operating push-pull trains on the Londonderry line, and by substituting for d.e.m.u.s on the Portadown-Bangor route.

Nonetheless, by the mid-1980s passengers on the Larne route were complaining about the state of their trains. The original 1966 diesel electric railcars had been split up into three-car sets with driving trailers rebuilt out of former NCC carriages that had seen several metamorphoses in their long lives. Tarting one up in an *ersatz* Sealink livery only helped to emphasise the dull appearance of the remainder. BREL came to the rescue with an exceptionally low-cost "new" train project.

New "half-price" trains
The idea was simple. Take a new carriage body to the standard BR suburban design, mount it on a sturdy second-hand BR mark 1 underframe and bogies, fit second hand power units and traction motors from redundant NIR units, and you have a half-price unit. Nine three-car sets were delivered between 1985 and 1987, six for the Larne line and three for services out of Belfast

Below: *Soon after its inauguration, by 1969 NIR had realised it could not survive without at least some locomotives! It bought three 620hp 0-6-0 diesel hydraulic shunting locomotives from English Electric at Newton-le-Willows for shunting and general trip work. All have recently been withdrawn, and all are held for preservation by the Irish Traction Group. No. 2 was photographed at Belfast central service depot on 16th May 1988.*

Above: *Major changes recently launched by Northern Ireland Railways in Belfast include the bridge over the River Lagan in Belfast that links the Larne line with the rest of the system, and the new city centre terminus station on the site of the former GNR one at Great Victoria Street, which is much more central than Central station. Class 80 d.e.m.u. power car No. 85 approaches the new terminus on a very frosty 6th December 1996 with the 08.25 from Bangor to Lisburn.*

Opposite: *One of the last two outposts of the formerly widespread somersault signals of the Belfast & Northern Counties Railway is the branch from Coleraine to Portrush. On rare occasions Portrush signal cabin is opened to handle special trains such as the RPSI's 'Portrush Flyer'. Otherwise it remains switched out, and the signals stand with their arms suspended in the "clear" position as shown: surely a classic design. On 22nd October 1983 a class 80 d.e.m.u. formed as a two-car unit arrives at Portrush from Coleraine. Working somersault signals can still be seen at Castlerock in 1997.*

Central. These were an instant success. One possibly unfortunate NIR promotion for shopping trips to Belfast earned the units the nickname "shopping trolleys", which is a pity. They offer a good quality suburban fleet, even though their start-to-stop performance is limited by the low power available.

NIR trains have sported more liveries than one would expect from such a small railway. NIR was sectorised in a business sense for a while in the mid-1980s, and each director, of course, wanted his own train colours. This happened just after the new grey-with-maroon-band colours had started appearing on the class 80 units. After the Monopolies and Mergers Commission report had criticised the sectorisation of such a small railway the passenger sectors were combined and new, more striking corporate colours appeared.

New bridge

In 1994 the Larne line was reconnected with the rest of the Irish rail network by means of the new bridge over the River Lagan in Belfast. York Road terminus was replaced by a small high level station, Yorkgate, on the new line. Larne trains can now run into Central station and continue to other destinations. The other big event of recent years has been the building of a new station at Great Victoria Street, fed through a triangular junction on to the Belfast union railway so that d.e.m.u.s can call at all Belfast stations on their route through (or rather round) the city centre. The locomotive hauled Dublin trains still miss calling at the new terminus at the time of writing.

One diversion in traction policy occurred in 1986 when NIR bought six displaced former C class Bo-Bos from CIÉ. These were for handling ballast and other engineers' trains. They were also to be held in readiness for some coal (lignite) traffic that was anticipated to arise from proposed workings near Antrim on the shores of Lough Neagh. The locomotives received NIR blue livery and numbers upwards from 104 inclusive. They did not prove entirely successful. The lignite traffic did not materialise, and all these locomotives are now withdrawn. Also withdrawn are two of the three Hunslet Bo-Bos. No. 102 survives as the allocated Adelaide yard pilot locomotive. ◆

14

The lord's railway - Shane's Castle

Imagine a deciduous wood - a bird sanctuary - a haunted castle - the largest freshwater lake in the United Kingdom - sun shining through the leafy boughs. Who could ask for more? Imagine, then, that this idyllic vision is not only reality, but that a delightful 3ft gauge steam railway meanders through it all. Until very recently this was so! Near Antrim, on Lord O'Neill's estate, ran the mile long Shane's Castle Railway, the purpose of which was to carry visitors from the estate gate to the castle area. Passengers paid to gain entry to the estate and the ride on the railway was free.

The Shane's Castle Railway presented the most shiny, clean steam locomotive the author had ever seen. No. 3 Shane was a large 0-4-0 well tank that had been built by Andrew Barclay of Kilmarnock as one of three steam locomotives for

Right: *The Shane's Castle Railway transferred visitors from the estate main gate to the area by the lough shore that includes the castle and other antiquities. On the last day of the 1984 season, Sunday 2nd September, the train stands at the terminus at the castle end of the railway ready to perform its first run back to the estate entrance. The locomotive is the third of a trio of 0-4-0 well tank engines that were supplied to Bord na Móna in 1964 by Andrew Barclay of Kilmarnock, and carries the number 3 and the name* Shane.

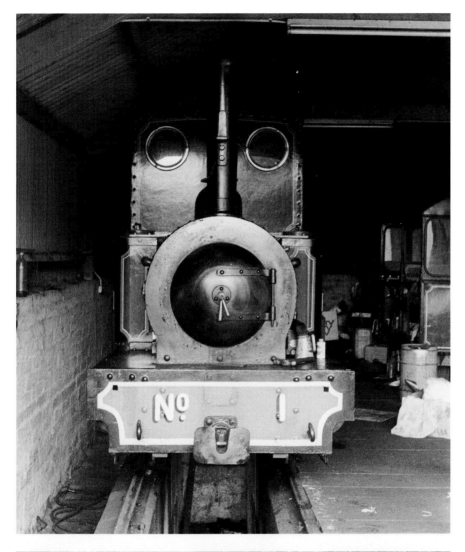

Left: *The locomotive stock on the Shane's Castle Railway included British Aluminium Company of Larne's 3ft gauge 0-4-0T No. 1, seen in the railway's locomotive depot on 2nd September 1984.*

Opposite: *Threading through woodlands and never far from the north shoreline of Lough Neagh, a trip on the Shane's Castle Railway on a sunny day was a delightful experience. The 0-4-0WT* Shane *crosses a stream on 2nd September 1984 as it makes its way with an afternoon train to the castle. The locomotive was liveried in a dark green with its exposed metalwork superbly burnished.*

the Bord na Móna turf-carrying rail system at Portarlington. For an organisation that normally only used diesel traction, the Turf Board steam purchase was somewhat unusual. The steam locomotives did not last long with the Board, and all three were sold off into preservation. Lord O'Neill's was the finest, even if its newly acquired chimney seemed a little too big for it.

Other traction on the line included No. 1 from the British Aluminium Company at Larne, a County Donegal 2-6-4T and an ore quarry engine from Northamptonshire. From time to time a County Donegal diesel railcar was seen to drive along the wooded track in the charge of its independent owners. The County Donegal items have since been moved to the museum in Londonderry.

Lord O'Neill's steam train usually shuttled up and down the line at weekends from late morning to early evening, through a season that lasted from spring to autumn. That it has been closed down is presumably a reaction to inevitable economic forces, but it passes with the regret of all who knew it during its relatively short life. ◆

Above: Shane *gallops alongside the roadway taking tourists who have visited the estate back to the entrance gate. This little railway ran in idyllic surroundings. While understanding the economic necessity, the author expresses his regret at Lord O'Neill's recent decision to close it down.*

15

Iarnród Éireann and the third diesel era

Irish Rail

CIÉ's railways became Iarnród Éireann (IÉ) in the mid 1980s, as part of the devolvement of management from the central body to its component parts. CIÉ as the holding company retained an overseeing role for IÉ and the different road transport groups.

As the English language is spoken much, much more in Ireland than is Irish Gaelic, the image makers coined the phrase "Irish Rail", and designed the classic IR symbol that at once also resembled a double track railway with a branch leading off it. Train liveries had previously settled down to an attractive variant of the gold and black colours that had held sway since the early 1960s, and all IR needed to do to improve the livery still further was to paint white bands between the gold and black areas. This brightened the trains much more than one would have first thought.

Politically, the use of English as the first choice for the emblem of an Irish company did not go down well with the government. IR subsequently had to change, and to adopt its Irish language version, Iarnród Éireann, together with a new IÉ badge, a process which began in 1994 and which is still far from complete. Thus there has been variety in liveries and badges for many years.

Second generation

By the early 1990s it was clear that the old Metro-Vick Co-Cos of the 001 class (the former A class) were not adequate for future freight loads nor

passenger train speeds. They were also approaching forty years old. Replacements were required. IÉ knew exactly where to look, in view of their happy association with General Motors, though they would have had to comply with the European rules about international

Above: *A new shape for a new vision is represented by the Co-Co class 201 locomotives of IÉ. With 3,200hp to deliver, a high tractive effort, and a maximum speed in excess of 100mph, the new GM locomotives exceed IÉ's current requirements, being built for the next forty years. No. 232 rests at Drogheda after arrival off the Dublin main line with a train of cement wagons and is standing at the beginning of the long branch to Navan and Kingscourt. Because of weight restrictions, a class 141 Bo-Bo took over the train before it could continue along the branch.*

competitive procurement. Doubtless GM's tender for the 34 new Co-Co locomotives was the most competitive, as by mid-1994 the company was scooping a world first by flying the initial locomotive of the new class to its customer, ostensibly to gain time for proving trials, but also a superb publicity stunt. No. 201 arrived in a Ukrainian bulk freight aeroplane, while its later colleagues had to endure the long Atlantic sea crossing from Canada. The first shipload came across in autumn 1994. The second ship brought the last 14 locomotives. The author witnessed one of these being unloaded on 25 March 1995. Two of the 34 locomotives were for Northern Ireland Railways.

The 201 class, surprisingly using up exactly the full number range of the former C class, are 3,200hp 100mph Co-Cos with modern, fuel

Above: *Unloading locomotives at a dockside nowadays is a simple process compared with years past. The "jumbo ship" that brought the last fourteen class 201 locomotives from Canada to Dublin was able to unload them using one of its two on-board cranes. Co-Co No. 206, well sheeted to deter the effects of the elements, is seen being unloaded at North Wall Quay, Dublin, on 25th March 1995 while class 141 Bo-Bo No. 143 waits to drag it to Inchicore for commissioning.*

Top Right: *New Co-Co No. 205 arrives at Dublin Heuston with the 07.35 from Cork on 25th March 1995. Liveried in smart orange livery, these locomotives carry the new Iarnród Éireann symbol. The coaching stock is mark 3 type in the Irish Rail style with additional white lining bands.* (Photo: Mrs. Mary Boocock)

Bottom Right: *Use of class 201 Co-Cos has enabled IÉ to increase the maximum weight of freight trains from 850 to 1,500 tonnes. A long, up container train passes through Kildare behind No. 205 on 9th May 1997.*

> ❝ THE OLD MAN *approached my wife and me as we stood on platform 1 at Dublin's Heuston station. Being in the open air, platform 1 was a particularly cold place to wait for a train to photograph on this icy March morning in 1995. "Is this where the Kildare train goes from?" he asked. "Yes," I replied. Trying to encourage him, I added, "And it's a new train!"*
>
> *"Everything is new!" he jested. "The last time I was here this was Kingsbridge, and now it's called Heuston. I always thought Euston was in London!"* ❞

Above: *Seventeen of these Japanese-built, suburban type, diesel hydraulic multiple unit vehicles were delivered to IÉ in 1994. Dubbed the "Arrow" trains, they work out of Dublin to Kildare, Maynooth, Drogheda and Dundalk. This unit is formed of cars 2611 and 2612, and is seen about to terminate at Kildare on the 08.00 from Dublin Heuston. This is a new service of suburban trains that began operation in 1994, designed to provide new travel opportunities for the several reopened stations at the Dublin end of the Cork main line.*

Top Right: *A class 201 Co-Co crosses the River Shannon bridge at Athlone with the 08.25 from Dublin Heuston to Westport on 5th December 1996. The main station for Athlone at the beginning of the period covered by this book was to the west of this bridge (ahead of the train shown here). By diverting trains for Galway and Westport to start from Heuston station in Dublin and run via Portarlington, CIÉ was able to reduce the Mullingar-Athlone line to freight only. CIÉ then closed the former MGWR Athlone station and modernised and reopened the smaller ex-GS&WR one nearer the town centre.*

efficient engines and electronically controlled wheel creep equipment for very high starting tractive effort. Their silencing is beyond the author's previous experience. It incorporates "negative sound generation", an electronic system that broadcasts sound waves opposite to those being produced by the engine, so blanking out much of the noise.

The 201 class locomotives are specified at a performance level beyond what is needed in Ireland now. They are capable of starting freight trains up to 3,000 tonnes weight, whereas IÉ intend to use them to increase Irish freight trains from 850 to 1,500 tonnes. In this way IÉ's engineers have provided the railway with locomotives that will cope with the increasing demands of the next forty years.

The 100mph-plus top speed is seeing early use. As part of the European Union's programme for high speed trunk railway routes, the Belfast-Dublin-Cork axis has been designated a route for refurbishment to 90-100mph operation with new track and signalling at places where the existing infrastructure does not support such speeds. IÉ has completed the bulk of the work on the Dublin-Cork section and 100mph services are planned for introduction in 1997. The purchase of the class 201 locomotives is the key to the rolling stock side of the equation. Fortunately the mark 2 and mark 3 coaching stock is designed to operate at these speeds.

Japanese imports

IÉ also wanted new diesel railcars for suburban and local services. This time the observant commentator might have identified the specification as matching that of a British Rail class

150/2 series "Sprinter". Again, the European open procurement process had to be followed, with a notice in the European Journal. Open competition resulted in a better bid from the Tokyu Car Co. of Japan. 17 cars entered service in 1994 and 1995, formed as two-car sets with one spare vehicle. Outwardly they are similar to the British 150s and could reasonably be dubbed the "Japanese Sprinters". They are gangwayed throughout and have suburban-style power-operated doors at the one-third and two-third bodyside positions. Each car has a Japanese hydraulic transmission driven from an underfloor Cummins 350hp diesel engine, geared for a maximum speed of 70mph.

Branded the "Arrow" trains, Japanese railcars can be seen on the new Dublin suburban route to Kildare for which a number of stations were opened or reopened on the main line out of Heuston station.

They also work the Maynooth trains, and a number of trains between Dublin Pearse and Drogheda or Dundalk. One is used between Cork and Cobh. There are also some Friday and Sunday InterCity duties for these trains.

Consequences

The arrival of the Arrow units has not completely cleared locomotive hauled working from the suburban and local services. GM Bo-Bos can still be seen at peak times on Dublin area workings; they also work the Ballina branch. Trains between Limerick, Ballybrophy and Limerick Junction use Bo-Bos and coaches, too. The amount of rolling stock used on an Irish locomotive hauled local train must be uneconomic. To provide a Bo-Bo diesel electric locomotive and a bogie heating van to move one or two Cravens coaches along a single track to shift a handful of passengers suggests that IÉ needs

yet more diesel multiple units.

As a result of Eire's "third wave" of dieselisation, all the former Metro-Vick locomotives were withdrawn, mostly for scrap. A few examples of the A and C classes are now preserved. IÉ had begun to withdraw the BRC&W B class back in the 1970s, their Sulzer engines making them non-standard for maintenance and overhaul. One of these is preserved also. ◆

Below: *The modern station nameboards used by IÉ are clear to read, but are less attractive without the stylish Gaelic lettering for the Irish version of the station names. Compare this with the photograph of the nameboard at the end of Chapter 1.*

16

To America and back - the Tralee & Dingle Railway

Blennerville remains a little-known village to most people. Many years ago, though, it had a part to play in the changing destinies of many Irish families. Located on the west coast of Ireland a few miles west of Tralee, Blennerville was one of the Atlantic ports from which Irish emigrants sailed on their desperate journeys to escape the effects of economic hardship.

Today, in an Ireland that for the first time knows widespread prosperity, Blennerville is a popular tourist location. It is also the centre of operation of the Tralee & Dingle Railway. This is not the cattle-carrying T&DR of the distant past, though there are some common features. Today's T&DR is totally a tourist operation. It has a tenuous connection at Tralee with the nearby IÉ railway, and takes visitors to a new terminus under the shadow of a windmill. Its route lies for the most part along the former 3ft gauge railway's track bed. There are new, major tourist complexes at each end of the line.

The railway's steam locomotive is an original from the older T&DR. Hunslet 2-6-2T No. 5 was the largest locomotive on the former railway, and was useful enough to be transferred to the Cavan & Leitrim section of CIÉ in 1949, a few years before the T&DR finally closed. No. 5T, as it was then, worked trains on the C&L's main line between Dromod and Ballinamore, and on to Belturbet (see the illustration in chapter 3). When the Cavan & Leitrim line closed down, No. 5T, together with C&L 4-4-0T No. 3L *Lady Edith*, was exported to the USA for preservation. Happily, the 2-6-2T is now back in Ireland, fully overhauled and restored to a fine, green livery, and plays its essential role as the centre of attraction on the new T&DR. We wish this venture well. ◆

Below: *This is the modern Tralee & Dingle Railway, a commercial enterprise enabling holidaymakers to travel between tourist attractions in west Tralee and Blennerville. Former T&DR 2-6-2T No. 5 has arrived at the new T&DR station in the shadow of the windmill at Blennerville on 11th March 1997, having followed for almost two miles the track bed of the former 3ft gauge line. This is actually now the most westerly railway station in Europe!*

Above: No. 5 rests at Blennerville after arrival from Tralee. The carriages were imported from a railway in Northern Spain, regauged, overhauled and fitted with public address equipment. Compare this portrait of No. 5 with the view of the same locomotive over forty years earlier in Chapter 3.

Right: The splendidly restored 2-6-2T No. 5 shuttles tourists hourly in the summer months over the short distance between Tralee Ballyard and Blennerville Windmill stations. It is seen here having crossed a minimal bridge over a stream on the original T&DR track bed.

17

Main line steam preserved - the RPSI

By far the most active independent railway preservation group in Ireland is the Railway Preservation Society of Ireland. The RPSI spans both Irish communities. Its main base is in the north, at Whitehead on the Larne branch. In the south is a smaller, though no less effective group whose activities centre on Mullingar. The key achievement of the RPSI is the establishment over many years of a regular programme of steam specials all over Ireland. Most of these specials are open to the general public at fares that appear very reasonable when compared with steam specials in the U.K.

The author first sampled one in 1984 when he and his friend Nick joined a Belfast to Dublin day excursion headed by former NCC 2-6-4T No. 4. Nicknamed a "Jeep" by the local enthusiasts, a name which derived from the immediate post-war delivery dates of the first batch of WT class engines, No. 4 was master of its task of taking eight, restored, plain-bearing carriages of various origins along the international main line. The leading vehicle was an old GNR saloon that was the personal vehicle of Lord O'Neill of Shane's Castle. Other coaches came from the GNR, the NCC and even the GS&WR. The buffet car was grandly lettered LMS - NCC and was a source of considerable refreshment to the

travellers during the day.

The flow of Guinness is also a feature of the annual weekend steam outings run by the RPSI. Usually starting on a May Saturday morning from Dublin, the weekend tour train runs to a destination decided on by RPSI members after the previous

year's tour. Trains have ended up variously at Rosslare, Limerick, Tralee, Galway, Sligo and Derry, to the author's knowledge. There is always a banquet at a good hotel on the Saturday evening. The second day sometimes features a run on a freight-only line, or an unusual

routing, and often ends up with a spirited run from Dublin to Belfast. The tours include run-pasts, and sometimes special buses are laid on to take enthusiasts to good locations for photographs and filming.

The RPSI make the most of all stock movements associated with the

Above: *During the Railway Preservation Society of Ireland's weekend tour on 15th May 1988, all eyes are on the blue compound 4-4-0 No. 85 as it stops at Drogheda for water on the last leg of the tour. The support coach is a splendid GS&WR 12-wheeled clerestory composite brake vehicle. Use of preserved carriages has since been banned on the Cork-Dublin and Dublin-Belfast main lines because each route has been upgraded for 90mph or 100mph running. Trains of IÉ Cravens stock are currently favoured for this duty.*

Left: *Run-pasts are a feature of the RPSI steam tours, sometimes to illustrate the train in interesting surroundings rather than climbing grades flat out. The popular "Jeep" class WT 2-6-4T No. 4 curves into Birdhill on the Ballybrophy-Limerick line, framed by standard CIÉ semaphore signals on 14th May 1988.*

Mullingar share a considerable volume of work in overhauling and repairing these valuable machines. In the author's opinion, they do extremely well to provide power for so many trains from such a relatively small stock. For one must not forget the summer seaside 'Portrush Flyer' trips, nor the December 'Santa specials', both of which operate out of Belfast, so the effort is an all-the-year-round one. (At the time of writing, following a derailment at speed for which the cause is being contested, no steam passenger trains are operating in Northern Ireland. We hope this situation will soon be resolved.)

The Mullingar centre has restored a 1950s CIÉ express corridor train set, one of the group with timber framed, steel clad bodies mounted on Commonwealth bogies. Painted in CIÉ light green, the set is a fine addition to the RPSI's fleet. Operation of all the restored vehicles on the main lines of Ireland is becoming difficult, however. As the principal routes are upgraded for higher speeds, only robust, steel coaches are permitted. Thus, when the steam specials operate between Dublin and Cork, or on the Dublin-Belfast line in Eire, a set of IÉ Cravens coaches is used. The Cravens vehicles are actually highly suitable, being vacuum braked and steam heated. The ability to open windows and top lights enables passengers to enjoy the smells and sounds of steam travel from inside the train, and yet to travel

"ON THE DAY steam excursion from Belfast to Dublin, running by 2-6-4T No. 4 was extremely brisk on the return journey between Drogheda and Dundalk. When the author and his friend Nick alighted at Belfast Central, the party in the buffet car was still going on. As the passengers walked along the platform to the slope that led to the concourse, loud singing from many voices still rocked the buffet car! We never did discover whether they all ended up in the carriage sidings, or how they were eventually persuaded to leave the train.**"**

weekend, and indeed other, trips. Extra fares are charged for those people who have not had enough and who want to stay with the train until it is finally stabled at Whitehead or Mullingar.

The locomotive stock of the RPSI includes two GNR 4-4-0s, Nos. 85 *Merlin* and 171 *Slieve Gullion*. There is the D&SER class K2 2-6-0 No. 461, and the NCC 2-6-4T No. 4. Most locomotives are based at Whitehead, including SL&NCR 0-6-4T *Lough Erne* and the Londonderry Port & Harbour Commissioners 0-6-0ST No. 3. The Mullingar team is responsible for the two GS&WR J15s, Nos. 184 and 186. The former is still unsuperheated.

The centres at Whitehead and

in relatively comfortable, roomy and smooth riding carriages. An act of inexcusable vandalism occurred in 1996 when three older carriages were set alight in the yard at Whitehead. Yet the full programme of runs was executed, despite the disappointment that that action caused.

There are a few other enthusiast groups in Ireland restoring locomotives for main line running. Mention must be made of the Irish Traction Group who are working to bring older diesel classes back into service to perpetuate former sights and smells. Metro-Vick Co-Co No. A39, now in CIÉ original silver livery, is one success though it sensibly retains a General Motors engine, as does Bo-Bo No. C231 which is in the CIÉ interim green.

The Great Southern Railway Preservation Society at Mallow is attempting to bring GNR class Q 4-4-0 No. 131 up to main line standard. Progress at Mallow is slow. Shortages of both funding and political will are leaving SL&NCR bogie railcar B and two classic six-wheeled coaches decaying seriously in the open air. At the time of writing, these treasures are seen to be in great danger.

There is some steam in Northern Ireland at summer weekends, at Downpatrick on a track bed of the former B&CDR. The Downpatrick Steam Railway operates one of the Guinness broad gauge saddle tanks, and is seen by some as a likely place for future running of SL&NCR 0-6-4T *Lough Erne*.

Another, smaller preservation centre is at Tuam, between Galway and Sligo. This team have restored to working order the tiny GS&WR 0-6-0T No. 90 that used to work on the Timoleague & Courtmacsherry branch, but this does not see regular running. ◆

Above: *Run-pasts are a feature of the RPSI May weekend railtours. Former Dublin & South Eastern Railway 2-6-0 No. 461 was photographed by a bus-load of enthusiasts as it headed west through pleasant countryside between Rathmore and Killarney on the Mallow-Tralee line on 10th May 1997. The Cravens coaches that the engine is hauling are receiving their steam heat from the generator van, a former British Rail brake second coach which CIÉ converted to a steam heat generator and brake van.*

Below: *From time to time the RPSI steam locomotives put up some highly creditable performances. Former GNR class S 4-4-0 No. 171 speeds through Donabate with a crackling roar on 12th May 1997 with the final train of the weekend tour special, bound for Dundalk. For a season, No. 171 was painted early GNR plain black and shorn of its* Slieve Gullion *nameplates. It is planned to revert to the attractive blue livery after its forthcoming overhaul.*

Left: *A feature of the RPSI annual weekend events is the sale of tickets to ride the special train on its positioning moves before and after the tour. On Monday 16th May 1988, No. 85 Merlin storms past Adelaide on its way from Belfast Central via Lisburn and Antrim to Portrush, the first leg of its move back to Whitehead.*

Right: *Some people have to work to keep the tour going! Four men and a fork lift truck at Limerick are employed to lift and discharge about twenty bags of American coal into the tender of unsuperheated class J15 0-6-0 No. 184 during the weekend tour on 14th May 1988 that rested at Limerick overnight. No. 184 is based at the RPSI's Mullingar centre.*

Above: *The site at Whitehead where the RPSI maintains and overhauls its northern locomotive fleet has plenty of covered accommodation, though it is always never enough. On 7th December 1996 Merlin is again being steamed, this time in readiness for the next day's two return 'Santa specials' to be operated out of Belfast Central. The 0-6-0 saddle tank preparing to make up the train at Whitehead is former Londonderry Port & Harbour Commissioners No. 3 R.H. Smyth. It carries builders' plates stating it was built by Peckett & Co. of Bristol in 1928 (works No. 2021), yet its appearance is clearly that of an Avonside-designed locomotive. Indeed the book,* ABC of Irish Locomotives (1) *tables this as an Avonside product.*

18

The international railway - renewal

The two Irish capital cities of Dublin and Belfast deserve something better than the investment-starved former GNR main line in the 1990s. This message got home to the European Commissioner responsible for transport. Now the route is seen as part of the grand European trunk route plan. This plan includes the links from Cork and Belfast via Dublin and Dun Laoghaire to Holyhead, Crewe and London, thence through the Channel Tunnel to the continent itself. So the European Community is supporting with hard cash a higher speed railway between Belfast, Dublin and Cork. The Belfast to Dublin section requires the greater amount of work (how times have changed since CIÉ in the distant past seemed so much less of a quality railway

Right: *Funded partly by grants from the European Union as part of the continent-wide network of railway trunk routes, the international Belfast-Dublin line is being rebuilt for higher speed running. At the same time as track renewals, the railways are resignalling the route and modernising the principal stations. This is Drogheda, having just lost its through track in the interests of providing wider platforms. Two IÉ class 121 single-cab Bo-Bos, Nos. 124 and 128, propel a ballast train through the main northbound platform on 12th May 1997.*

Left: *On 19th October 1992, NIR GM Co-Co No. 113* Belfast & Co. Down *arrives at Drogheda with the 11.00 from Dublin Connolly to Belfast, in the days when the middle track was still regularly used. An outer suburban train of IÉ Cravens coaches bound for Dublin is leaving the opposite platform behind an IÉ class 141 Bo-Bo, while an engineers' train waits in the centre road.*

Above: *As a first step towards improving the Belfast-Dublin main line services, both IÉ and NIR received deliveries of new 3,200hp class 201 GM Co-Co locomotives in 1994 and 1995. Four of them were equipped with push-pull equipment to work with the new train sets to be delivered from de Dietrich in 1996 and 1997. These locomotives were Nos. 206 and 207 owned by IÉ, and 208 and 209 which went to NIR. The four locomotives were initially in the standard liveries of the railways concerned. Before the new trains were in service, the locomotives were used with the existing coaching stock sets. Here is NIR No. 209 approaching Belfast Adelaide on the 09.30 from Belfast Central to Dublin Connolly on 6th December 1996.*

Above: *Another view of Drogheda that shows the civil engineering works being undertaken, particularly widening of the island platform on the right. On 12th May 1997, IÉ Co-Co No. 223 arrives with the 11.00 Belfast-Dublin.*

than did the Great Northern).

Most of the track and signalling work in the republic has been completed at the time of writing, and tenders have been let for the last track section in the north, namely that from Lisburn to Belfast Central. Operations using GNR semaphore signals came to an end in late spring 1997 with the abandonment and removal of the last pocket on the main line at Dunleer. Trackwork is now predominantly continuously welded rail on concrete sleepers with deep, stone ballast.

There is a new, rationalised track layout at Drogheda. By lifting the centre through track between the main up and down platforms, there is now room for realignment of the platform tracks to enable the main line platforms to be widened. As at many IÉ stations, the appearance of platform surfaces benefits from the laying of new brick tiles. The station rebuilding at Drogheda makes good use of the architecturally excellent features of the old station while presenting a much more modern image to the traveller. Similar modernisation is improving other stations on the route such as Dundalk.

The French rolling stock manufacturer de Dietrich has delivered four seven-coach push-pull sets of modern style and considerably enhanced comfort. The carriages are 23 metres long, and have a body profile identical to that adopted for the Channel Tunnel Eurostar trains. Internally they set a good standard for comfort.

New class 201 GM Co-Co locomotives No. 206 to 209 will power these trains. 208 and 209 belong to NIR, the others to IÉ. All will carry a common livery. The locomotives are named after the same rivers as were the former GNR class VS 4-4-0s also numbered 206 to 209!

These 100mph, air-conditioned train sets represent the best example of co-operation between the railways of the two countries for many, many years. Their launch into service, planned for 1st September 1997, gives eight trains each way each day, by far the best service in recent memory on that beleaguered main line. ◆

Right: *A new image has been created for the international trains, using the well-known 'Enterprise' brand name.*

Above: *Two generations of trains on the Belfast-Dublin route are seen at Dublin Connolly on the evening of 14th May 1997. On the right is NIR Co-Co No. 113* Belfast & Co. Down *at the head of the 18.20 to Dublin, formed of NIR mark 2 pressure-ventilated stock. IÉ class 201 Co-Co No. 206* River Liffey *stands in platform 1 with a short test train of the new push-pull stock that was programmed to begin the new enhanced service between the capital cities on 1st September 1997, at about the same date as this book was due to be published.*

Below: *A fine landmark on the international railway is the magnificent Boyne Bridge at Drogheda. A NIR class 111 Co-Co crosses the bridge on 19th October 1992 with the 15.00 from Belfast Central to Dublin Connolly.* (Photo: Mrs Mary Boocock)

19

Preservation in Donegal (and elsewhere)

Two small bodies have considered opening short lengths of 3ft gauge track on the former track beds of parts of the County Donegal Railway. One is situated on the former Glenties branch, and the other is centred on a museum at the former CDRJC station in Donegal.

The Central Gaeltacht Train Society has opened a stretch of the CDRJC Glenties route along the shores of Lough Finn from Fintown.

The ultimate aim is to reopen the track through to Glenties. This railway is essentially a tourist operation. Traction is a small Simplex internal combustion locomotive, and the carriages are old tramcars from Charleroi in Belgium. Trains run daily from June to September, and there are Santa specials in December.

One cannot fail to be encouraged by the enthusiasm of the young ladies who man the Donegal Railway Heritage Centre, a small museum set out in part of the former CDRJC station in Donegal town. Even though most of the people involved in this project are too young to remember the County Donegal Railway, they have put together (no doubt with good advice from older

locals who do remember!) an excellent collection of models, photographs and artefacts from the old CDR, and also a selection from the Londonderry & Lough Swilly Railway. Outside the museum is a carriage brake van body that has been restored to the glorious red-and-cream livery of the CDR. Work is also under way in restoring a CDR diesel railcar.

Hidden away behind the bus garage is the heavily tarpaulined hulk of CDRJC 2-6-4T No. 5 *Drumboe*. This locomotive stood in the open air for nearly forty years, and the ravages of weather, time and vandals have taken their toll. Nonetheless, this treasure of an engine is safe, and presents an expensive challenge to anyone determined to restore it to future

Below: *The Donegal Railway Heritage Centre uses the west wing of the former CDRJC station building at Donegal, that is the single storey section on the left of this view. Bus Éireann occupies the rest of the buildings*

operation. The supporting society have a gleam of a distant idea that they would like to open a short part of the CDR Ballyshannon branch.

The passenger on a down Sligo express train who looks out as the train leaves Dromod will see part of the small rolling stock collection of the new Cavan & Leitrim Railway. Using a restored steam locomotive from overseas, trains are run at weekends. The ultimate aim is to get the working railway going as far as Mohill, the largest town in the area served by the former C&LR. ◆

Above: *This excellent model, a star exhibit in the Donegal Railway Heritage Centre, accurately depicts the CDR station at Donegal in its heyday. Railcar 10 stands at the eastbound platform while 2-6-4T No. 5 Drumboe arrives from the direction of the Barnesmore Gap. The tracks to the right lead off in the direction of Killybegs. (The station buildings and the bus garage as depicted in the model are still there today. The rusty hulk of* Drumboe *now stands behind the bus garage awaiting restoration.)*

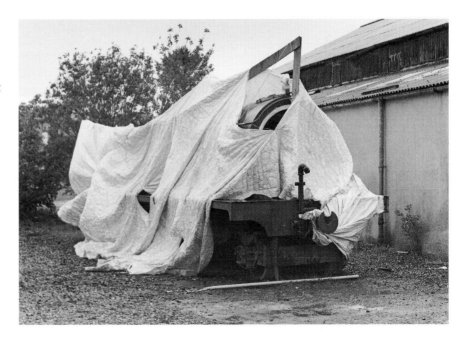

Right: *After forty years of advancing dereliction in the open air, CDRJC 2-6-4T No. 5 Drumboe was moved early in 1997 to Donegal, near the Donegal Railway Heritage Centre, where it is seen on 7th May 1997 at least partially protected by plastic sheeting.*

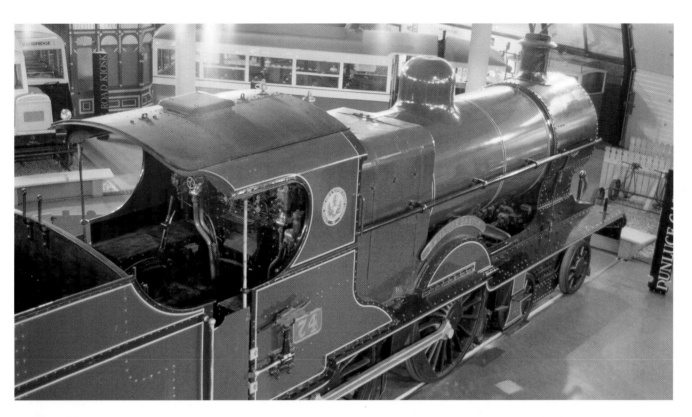

20

Museums

Above: *To many, the star exhibit at Cultra is the former NCC class U2 4-4-0 No. 74* Dunluce Castle, *restored resplendent in Midland crimson lake livery. This view, taken from the gallery above the railway section of the museum on 6th December 1996, clearly shows the livery details and also the automatic tablet catching apparatus on the cab side.*

Opposite: *The largest railway exhibit in the Ulster Folk and Transport Museum at Cultra is former GSR E.C. Bredin class B1a 4-6-0 No. 800* Maedb *which used to ply between Dublin and Cork. This class surely represents the zenith of successful steam locomotive development in Ireland.*

Below: *Although small in area, the Foyle Valley Railway museum in Londonderry has enough fascinating exhibits to occupy an enthusiast for half a day at least. County Donegal railcar No. 18 (left) stands opposite the same railway's 2-6-4T No. 6* Columbkille.

No-one should miss visiting the Ulster Folk and Transport Museum in Cultra, accessed directly from the station of that name on the Bangor line. The museum is worth spending a day at because of its wide variety of exhibitions. Be prepared to admire the ancient trams, the old cars (I remember when many were new!), and the beautifully restored buses and motorcycles. Do not miss the marine section dedicated to Belfast-built ships, including the very moving display that commemorates the loss of the *Titanic*.

But dwell particularly in the new hall that contains the railway

exhibits. *Maedb*, No. 800, is there standing grandly alongside the Londonderry Port & Harbour Commissioners 0-6-0ST No. 1. To the author, the star exhibit is the superbly restored NCC 6ft-wheeled 4-4-0 No. 74 *Dunluce Castle*, rightly placed in the central position. There is GNR 2-4-2T No. 93, a Guinness 1ft 10in gauge 0-4-0T, CDRJC 2-6-4T No. 2 *Blanche*, British Aluminium 0-4-0T No. 2, graceful Cavan & Leitrim 4-4-0T No. 2, and a nicely painted Portstewart Tramway engine which is also No. 2. The old GNR railbus stands alongside B&CDR 4-4-2T No. 30, not far from the much more modern BREL railbus that NIR used for a few seasons in the early 1980s on the Portrush branch. CDR diesel railcar No. 10 is there, as is No. 11 *Phœnix*. The oldest railcar is CDR No. 1 that dates back to 1906!

The visitor to Ireland should also see the new narrow gauge museum at Londonderry. This is situated on the site of the former GNR station at Foyle Road. A short stretch of 3ft gauge track is being laid along the former GNR broad gauge route in the Strabane direction. Called the Foyle Valley Railway, the line will hopefully soon extend up to eight miles, all on the opposite bank of the River Foyle to the old NCC 3ft gauge line that

Left: *The Foyle Valley Railway is laying its 3ft gauge track along the bed of the former GNR Derry main line. The aim is to extend the railway across the border into Eire. By May 1997, the line had extended to over three miles length: CDRJC railcars 18 (nearest) and 12, operating back-to-back, were photographed standing at the current extremity of the railway.*

Below: *Built in 1891 by Robert Stephenson & Co., 0-6-0ST No. 1 of the Londonderry Port & Harbour Commissioners stands in the Ulster Folk and Transport Museum on 6th December 1996. The locomotive was used to shunt the wagons of the various railways that used the docks in Derry, and consequently has couplings for narrow gauge (3ft) as well as broad gauge wagons.*

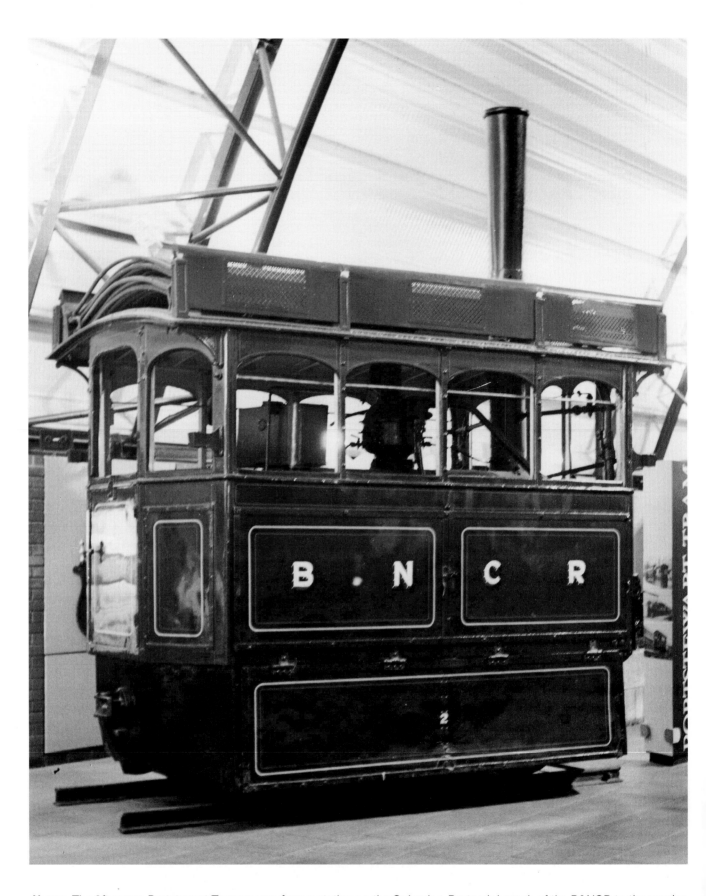

Above: *The 3ft gauge Portstewart Tramway ran from a station on the Coleraine-Portrush branch of the B&NCR to the nearby town of Portstewart. Of its three tram engines, only No. 2, built by Kitson in 1883, survives in Ireland. It is displayed in the Ulster Folk and Transport Museum at Cultra.*

Above: *The Foyle Valley Railway occupies part of the site of the GNR's Foyle Road terminus in Londonderry. After years in dereliction, CDRJC 2-6-4T No. 4* Meenglas *was rescued, cosmetically painted red, and placed on a short track outside the museum to act as a visual attraction for the site. Restoration of No. 4 is a long-term project.*

Right: *This scene in the railway section of the Ulster Folk and Transport Museum at Cultra shows (left) GNR 2-4-2T No. 93, (background) NCC 4-4-0 No. 74* Dunluce Castle *and (right) CDRJC 2-6-4T No. 2* Blanche. *This is a relatively new building, purpose-designed for the exhibition of railway equipment.*

the CDRJC operated until 1954. Nowadays it is the new line that sees CDR power in the form of two most beautifully restored Gardner-Walker articulated diesel railcars, Nos. 18 and 12 operating back-to-back. CDRJC 2-6-4Ts Nos. 4 *Meenglas* and 6 *Columbkille* are also here, having been recovered from dereliction. One looks forward to the possibility that one or other of these beautiful engines may eventually see active service again on this track.

The Foyle Valley Railway aims to open its narrow gauge line right across the border to Carrigans in the republic. When they succeed, they will have produced the first international preserved railway in the British Isles! ◆

> **❝ THE CLOGHER VALLEY** *Railway ran along the road from Augher to Clogher and Fivemiletown. Fivemiletown is a very snobby place. The people on one side of the road don't talk to the people on the other side. That's because on the other side of the road is the cemetery." (These were the opening sentences of a lecture to the Bournemouth Railway Club on the Clogher Valley Railway by Irish railway historian Dr. Donald McNeill.)* ❞

21

Turf for power - the Bord na Móna railways

If ever a country kept a railway secret for thirty years it was Ireland. Sometimes, the existence of the Irish turf railways was hinted at from the occasional sightings by rail travellers of pairs of shiny narrow gauge rails disappearing under main line railway bridges, but the attractions of the passenger carrying main railways diverted railway students' attention away from these. Thus it was only late in 1996 that the author became significantly aware of the totality of the Bord na Móna (Turf Board) narrow gauge railway networks when he bought a small book that listed the systems' locomotives and railcars (7).

Seventeen percent of the surface area of Ireland is bog land. This is particularly prevalent in the middle basin of Ireland, stretching westwards from not far from Dublin to reach almost to the Atlantic coast, and a similar distance north to south. The peat (the Irish call it "turf") is anything from a few feet to 50 feet deep. About seven percent of this bog land is actually owned by Bord na Móna, and forms the basis of the Irish turf industry. There are three main products: block peat for domestic use; milled peat for feeding modern power stations; and garden peat (Irish Moss Peat is a familiar export product). Earlier power stations such as that at Portarlington

used crudely cut "sod" peat. Two of these are now closed.

The major usage of peat is for power station fuel. Five turf-burning power stations are dotted around the countryside. These generate twelve per cent of the republic's electricity. Transporting the 5 million tonnes

annually of peat from the bogs to the power stations is the job of Bord na Móna's railways, all but one of which are the standard Irish 3ft narrow gauge. One 2ft gauge system survives, isolated from the rest at Glenties in County Donegal. This is now a workers' co-operative.

The author visited the Blackwater system in 1996. He discovered that there are something like 45 miles of permanent tracks there and about 50 miles of temporary tracks. (Across Ireland there are up to 1,200 miles of Bord na Móna railways!) The peat is milled during the summer months,

Above: *More than 17% of Ireland's land surface comprises peat bog. 7% of this is farmed by Bord na Móna, largely for power station fuel. A train of milled peat (the Irish call it "turf") traverses the Blackwater raised bog en route to Shannonbridge power station on 4th December 1996. The locomotive is one of the successful fleet of 3ft gauge Hunslet "Wagonmaster" 0-4-0 diesel mechanical locomotives, most of which have 85hp Ford engines. This industrial railway system runs up to fifty trains a day to Shannonbridge, each delivering about 75 tonnes of peat in its 15 bogie wagons.*

Left: *Bord na Móna peat trains are seen at Shannonbridge power station on 4th December 1996. The loaded train on the left, hauled by Hunslet locomotive No. LM386, approaches the station's twin wagon tipplers, while a train of empties passes on its way back to the Blackwater bog.*

Below: *A wagon is tippled in one of the two tipplers at Shannonbridge power station, Co. Offaly. Each wagon is turned over through 360° for complete discharge. On the left between the rails is the haulage chain that moves the train by stages, enabling each wagon to be emptied automatically.*

the top half inch or so being removed at each pass. The peat is then spread out in long ridges to dry out, to reduce as far as possible the water content which is initially as high as 80%. Temporary railway tracks are laid alongside the ridges of dried peat when loading is to take place. These tracks lead to the permanent tracks that link all the sites together and to the double track "main line" that leads to the power station.

The Blackwater railway system feeds the power station at Shannonbridge, a large station capable of outputting 125 Megawatts, and needing around one million tonnes of peat a year to do it. An average of fifty loaded trains a day are run, each taking up to 75 tonnes of

peat in fifteen bogie tippler wagons. On arrival at Shannonbridge, the small diesel locomotive is released from a loaded train, runs through one of the two rotary wagon tipplers, to collect an empty train. Meanwhile an automatic underground chain between the rails engages with the underside of the leading wagon. The train is taken through the tippler, and each wagon is turned over through 360°, dropping its load into an underground hopper. From there the turf is conveyed by belt to the power station.

There are several types of four-wheeled diesel locomotives in use. Most of the earliest, delivered in the 1960s and 1970, are small Rustons. Hunslet then came on the scene and

Above: *On 8th May 1997, Hunslet Wagonmaster 0-4-0 diesel mechanical No. LM 251 approaches Bellacorick power station, County Mayo, with a train of turf from the Oweninny No. 1 peat bog, a type known as blanket bog by virtue of its origin.*

Top Right: *Earlier locomotives used by Bord na Móna included many built by Ruston, such as Nos. LM151 (right) and LM128, at Blackwater on 4th December 1996.*

Bottom Right: *A 2ft gauge bog railway system exists near Glenties in County Donegal. This view at the main depot area on 7th May 1997 shows 45-year-old Ruston locomotive No. LM198 adjacent to a string of typical open-sided "sod peat" wagons. This system and its peat workings were recently transferred from Bord na Móna operation to a workers' co-operative.*

for a while provided what became the standard Bord na Móna locomotive, known as the Wagonmaster. These are 0-4-0 machines with jack-shaft drive and Ford engines. The latest locomotives are an hydraulic drive development, also designed by Hunslet specifically to meet Bord na Móna's requirements. Some of these were actually built in Bord na Móna's own workshops and have Cummins engines. There are a few other types, and several varieties of diesel powered inspection cars or personnel carriers. Many of the separate systems have their own locomotive liveries, or at least local variations.

Two Bord na Móna systems opened up parts of their enterprises to the public. Regular tourist trains are run during the summer season at Blackwater (about twelve miles south of Athlone) on what is called the Clonmacnoise & West Offaly Railway. There is a visitors' centre at Blackwater and lots of information, so this location makes an excellent family outing as well as being something different for the railway enthusiast to do.

At Bellacorick (twenty-odd miles west of Ballina) the passenger tours used a former West Clare section diesel railcar carriage (No. 3386) hauled by a Ruston locomotive, but low demand led to tours ceasing there at the end of the 1996 season.

According to a Bord official, there are at least 40 years worth of untapped turf available for electricity generation, so the sight of shiny narrow gauge rails disappearing under main line rail bridges will still puzzle travellers in Ireland for a long time into the future. ◆

22

The years to come

W hat will the next forty years hold for the railways of Ireland? The possibilities are endless.

New IÉ d.m.u.s

Certainly there are 27 new Arrow diesel railcars to be delivered soon. These are expected to come from GEC/Alsthom, and will probably be built in Spain. They will multiple freely with the existing Japanese railcars. These new trains ought to be enough to eliminate the uneconomic, short, locomotive hauled trains that still exist. Thus one can expect d.m.u.s to work all non-push-pull local trains on the lines out of Limerick, and also to add to the efforts of the Dublin outer-suburban push-pull trains. Some of these trains will run through from Drogheda to Arklow. Whether these purchases will allow for further expansion of local services in the potentially buoyant future economy of Eire will depend on many other factors that cannot be accurately foreseen now.

IÉ InterCity

Still in use are several peak main line trains of 1963 Cravens vehicles. These coaches are more than thirty years old and are steam heated. It is probably in the InterCity market that the greatest scope for future expansion lies. So for these two reasons one can expect IÉ to be in the

market again for additional InterCity-style coaching stock. This has already started, in 1996, with the putting into Galway line service of the former BREL 'International' train coaches.

The older GM locomotives have plenty of life left in them, so one can expect to see most of the 141 and 181 classes soldiering on for a decade at least, with twenty years a realistic life expectation for the class 071 Co-Cos. Even some of the oldest GM Bo-Bos, the single-cab class 121s, are being overhauled for further use on engineering and freight trains.

NIR replacements

The twenty-one units of the class 80 d.e.m.u. design were the subject of world-wide exploratory replacement market searches by NIR engineers before the merger with Ulsterbus. Since then, all has gone quiet. At twenty-three years old, the class 80s are not at their lives' end in engineering terms, though they do need attention to body corrosion and one can anticipate B.5 bogie frame cracks to be a problem by now. One can expect NIR to take a view on whether one more heavy overhaul

Above: *A major improvement to Northern Ireland's railway network was the opening in 1994 of the new bridge over the River Lagan in Belfast. The railway across this bridge linked Belfast Central station directly with a new through station (Yorkgate) near the former Belfast York Road terminus. Thus the Larne route was joined to the rest of the passenger network for the first time. On 14th May 1997, a class 80 d.e.m.u. crosses the bridge, which is known as the Dargan bridge after the famous Irish early railway engineer.*

would put off the date when fleet replacement is necessary, in which case orders for new diesel multiple units could be expected.

In the short term, the 4SRKT power units supplied in eight of the nine Castle class d.e.m.u.s are ageing, having been fitted second-hand from the 1966-built class 70 units. Following introduction of the new Belfast-Dublin trains, some respite for the d.e.m.u.s could possibly be had from limited re-introduction of locomotive hauled trains on the Londonderry route. Also, if the

Bleach Green route were to be re-opened with faster timings it should be possible to reduce the number of train sets needed to operate the service. So one could anticipate a strategy move to eliminate the earliest 4SRKT power units by

withdrawal of some of the worst of the class 80 units.

But the early mark 2 stock is itself coming up to thirty years old, and some move to replace it early in the next century can be expected. In the interim, IÉ might possibly consider

Above: *The Bleach Green route between Belfast and Antrim used to be set up for fast running. This view shows the semi-derelict Bleach Green route as seen from a Londonderry-Belfast d.e.m.u. that is diverging on to the Lisburn line. One looks forward to this route being recommissioned for fast running again, so that Derry can have a competitive train service once more.*

bidding for this potentially displaced NIR mark 2 stock. NIR itself would be likely to replace these trains with new diesel multiple units, possibly at the same time as they replace the class 80 units.

DART extensions

Extensions to the north and to the south are planned. The most eagerly awaited extension will be the southerly one around Bray Head to Greystones. This is currently a missing link in the suburban railway network, following the cessation of the old push-pull shuttle train from Bray. The proposed northerly extension to Malahide would bring the DART trains within earshot of Dublin's international airport - but what connection mode, if any, would be appropriate?

Light rapid transit

Funding has at last been agreed for the first stage of the proposal to build a light rapid transit system (known as LUAS) to take up the suburban corridors not adequately covered by heavy rail around Dublin. Two linked routes from the south are planned, one of which will use part of the former D&SER track bed on the Harcourt Street line. The other route will come from Tallaght in the south-west. This will provide a direct and straight service between Heuston station and the city centre, a link that is long overdue. An option for a route to the north-west would be in virgin railway territory and is not yet listed for funding. On-street running will be the norm in the inner city areas. The government has rejected proposals for underground sections on grounds of high cost. IÉ advise that the tramcars of the type known as

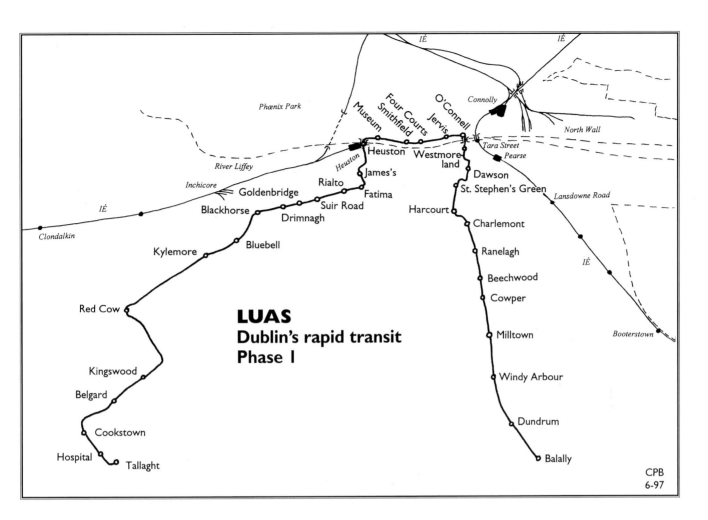

LUAS
Dublin's rapid transit
Phase 1

Phœnix Park

River Liffey

Inchicore

Clondalkin

IÉ

Goldenbridge

Blackhorse

Drimnagh

Kylemore

Bluebell

Red Cow

Kingswood

Belgard

Cookstown

Hospital

Tallaght

Museum

Smithfield

Four Courts

Jervis

O'Connell

Connolly

North Wall

Heuston

Westmore land

Tara Street

Pearse

James's

Rialto

Fatima

Suir Road

Dawson

St. Stephen's Green

Lansdowne Road

Harcourt

Charlemont

Ranelagh

Beechwood

Cowper

Milltown

Booterstown

IÉ

Windy Arbour

Dundrum

Balally

CPB
6-97

Above: *Phase 1 of the LUAS tram system for Dublin provides two linked routes as shown. In Phase 2, a third is proposed from the north-west of the city.*

Below: *IÉ have announced funding for their proposal to electrify the tortuous railway around Bray Head so that DART services can reach Greystones. An abandoned tunnel in this view (right) illustrates one of several early deviations from the original Brunel route that were necessary as a result of the combined effects of sea and cliff erosion. The train is an afternoon Rosslare-Dublin express headed by a class 071 Co-Co.*

Citadis have been selected from those offered by GEC/Alsthom, the preferred bidder.

Infrastructure

It is obvious to railway travellers in Ireland that there is still much jointed track in use, and that many areas are signalled by mechanical signals. To fund replacement of these is expensive, and would need to be done on an area basis, at least as far as signalling is concerned. The case to be made is usually that the railways can save high costs by the elimination of frequently sited mechanical signal cabins and by closure or replacement by modern barrier equipment of the many permanently-manned level crossings.

Above: *Future developments on IÉ include modernisation of principal stations. A good example is the work already done to provide a new station at Rosslare Harbour, listed in the timetable as Rosslare Europort. This view shows the tiled platform and new main building in May 1997. The bridge over the train brings passengers on the long walk from the ferries from Fishguard or Brittany. (The former station was actually much more convenient in its immediate location alongside the ship berths, but had virtually none of the amenities that passengers demand today.)*

Lightly-used routes such as those to Rosslare, Galway, Westport, Ennis, Sligo or Ballina might benefit from application of radio-controlled, possibly signal-less operation. Or at least the extension of centralised traffic control (CTC) with multiple aspect signalling could be useful. Semaphore signals have just been taken out of service at Dunleer to eliminate mechanical signalling on the Dublin-Belfast main line.

In Northern Ireland, replacement of the former B&NCR somersault signals on the Londonderry route at Castlerock, and of those on the Portrush branch, will no doubt be programmed soon.

Track replacement tends to be channelled into schemes that benefit the line speed of the route. Thus one can expect the old, jointed rails to continue as the norm for secondary lines. This is no hardship so long as the rolling stock is designed to take into account the potential alignment deficiencies of older track. Indeed, Irish bogie carriages have for decades been ideal for this use. The state of much of NIR's track, however, begs attention.

Stations

Schemes to brighten up IÉ's principal stations are led by the conviction that a welcoming entrance to the railway system is good for passenger business. Money has been made available for this, including Heuston and its grand main building. Tiled platform surfaces are becoming the norm.

With all this activity, one can see a happy future for Ireland's railways. They certainly deserve it: they have come a long way in the last forty years! ◆

Above: *For how long will it be necessary to guard sites such as Belfast Central station from the potential activities of terrorists? The high fencing that surrounds the main Belfast stations does nothing to improve their customer-attractiveness. No. 111* Great Northern *stands at Belfast Central with the 09.00 to Dublin on 1st September 1984. A class 80 d.e.m.u. waits on a Bangor train on the left.*

Epilogue

In forty years the railways of Ireland have moved a long way forward. Particularly in the republic, there has been a drive to eliminate old, expensive practices and equipment and to present to the passengers the face of a pleasant, user-friendly travel medium. Likewise, freight transit has been cut to the bone to take maximum advantage of rail's ability to move bulk loads efficiently.

The fortunes of the railways have in a way progressed hand-in-hand with the fortunes of the respective countries. When the author first visited Eire in 1956, he was confronted by begging children, barefoot in the streets of Dublin, the first beggars he had ever seen. In those days, Eire was still a poor country. Northern Ireland, by contrast, had an economy similar to that in the U.K., and always seemed to be more prosperous. Nowadays we see beggars in London; rarely now do we see them in Dublin or Belfast.

Today both countries are booming. Eire has benefited substantially as a result of its positive activity within the European Union, to the extent that its gross domestic product per head is said to be approaching that of the U.K. The removal of some of Eire's special financial advantages is expected shortly. On the other hand, Northern Ireland has been a beleaguered country in one respect, having to face the activities of terrorists. The province has had to be financially supported substantially by the United Kingdom government, for good reason more than have Scotland and Wales.

Terrorist activity has had its effects on the operation and economics of the railways in Ireland. Trains have been blown up (quite often CIÉ ones), particularly on the Belfast-Dublin main line. From time to time there have been bombs placed on the international railway track. Bomb threats have been a nuisance at the Belfast stations in particular. NIR have on occasions sent bomb-damaged rail vehicles to British railway works for repair. At least two CIÉ diesel locomotives were destroyed beyond repair.

The people of Northern Ireland have faced these actions, imposed on

Above: *Much more co-operation between the countries north and south of the border has developed in recent years. Rail freight services to Northern Ireland use IÉ trains throughout. A short container train heads on to the famous Boyne Bridge at Drogheda on 19th October 1992, hauled by GM Bo-Bo No. 192.*

them by a small minority, with stoicism and a desire to continue life as normal. Nowadays the shopping centres and factories of Belfast and other cities are thronged by people of both "communities", nationalist and loyalist. The division of the province into housing areas devoted to the different groups, however, and the separate schooling that many children receive, does little to foster understanding between them. The author finds this immeasurably sad. He has a deep love for the Irish people, irrespective of their political or religious persuasion. They have always treated him, his wife and his friends kindly, with good humour and with an open friendliness that is less common within the U.K. itself.

Yet in Eire, catholic and protestant people live side by side and their churches are often near or across the road from one another. In Eire the differences seem to mean nothing. The people in the republic prove that tolerance works, and that the divisions which so harm relationships within Northern Ireland are, if anything, man made and artificial. One could highlight the work of the Railway Preservation Society of Ireland as an example of good and supportive co-operation between the two countries. So also is the new Belfast-Dublin train service.

One cannot help feeling that a divided island community is always a compromise with the ideal. Ireland will eventually be re-united, that must be true. But, as the British government frequently states, this can only take place when the majority of people in Northern Ireland want it. That would presumably mean Sinn Fein and possibly the SDLP between them acquiring at a general election a majority of Northern Irish seats in the U.K. parliament, and then agreeing, presumably, to hold a referendum in the province (however unlikely all this may seem at the present time).

Does the present campaign of

terrorism help to achieve a united Ireland? This author fails to understand how it can. If anything is designed to cause British people to resist change, it is violence of this kind. It is probably becoming unlikely that a solution to the "Irish problem" (as former British prime minister William Gladstone described it) will come from the British side of the Irish Sea.

Could the European ideal of a common market with a common currency and more centralised sovereignty be of help? Possibly it could, but we are a long way from the federal structure that might enable this, and there are many voices against that in the U.K. at least.

In the end, the author believes, the solution rests upon the people of Ireland, all of them, on both sides of the border. When Jesus Christ was asked to define the two most important commandments, he said that we should love God with all one's heart, soul, strength and mind; and love one's neighbour as one's self. (See Luke's gospel, chapter 10, verse 27 in any edition of the Holy Bible). These commandments transcend all Christian "religious" denominations, whether catholic, protestant, anglican, "free", baptist, pentecostal, or whatever. If one loves one's self sufficiently to preserve one's own life, and obeys Christ's commandments, then how can the violence continue?

We must pray that the next forty years in Ireland are not troubled as have been the past 400. We must pray for reconciliation between the two "communities" in Northern Ireland. And we must pray that the trust that comes from mutual love and understanding will lead the Irish people to a permanently, peaceful and ultimately united existence. ◆

Above: *For twenty years at least, Dublin-Belfast trains have not had to change engines at Dundalk! On 13th May 1988, the IÉ 18.00 'Enterprise' service from Belfast Central arrives at Dublin Connolly headed by class 071 Co-Co No. 080. NIR No. 112* Northern Counties *awaits departure with the 20.00 to Belfast. The replacement trains introduced in 1997 have a common design and livery.*

Above: *A new image is being presented for the trains for the joint service between Dublin and Belfast, operated by both NIR and IÉ. The image is launched under the 'Enterprise' name, and the train livery is the same irrespective of which is the owning railway. Locomotive No. 206* River Liffey *shows the new colours. The new service of regular and fast push-pull trains was due to be inaugurated on 1st September 1997.*

Bibliography

1: A comprehensive source of basic information on Irish steam locomotives that the author relied on throughout all his early visits to Ireland is *The ABC of Irish Locomotives* by R.N. Clements and J.M. Robbins, published by Ian Allan Ltd. in 1949.

2: Readers may obtain up-to-date data on Irish diesel locomotives, railcars and carriages in the *European Handbook No. 7, Irish Railways Locomotives and Coaching Stock*, by Peter Fox, published 1996 by Platform 5 Publishing Ltd., ISBN 1 872524 82-6.

3: In 1966 Pan Books published Patrick J. Flanagan's detailed and entertaining account *The Cavan & Leitrim Railway*, ISBN 0 330 029428. It is definitive in its historical cover and in its descriptions of the route and its locomotives and rolling stock. It's good!

4: The poem by Percy French is quoted in full (with permission from the then owners of the copyright) in H. Fayle's book *The Narrow Gauge Railways of Ireland,* published in 1946 by W.P. Griffith & Sons Ltd. The book contains much, well-researched information on all of Ireland's narrow gauge railways up to its publication date. It is illustrated by photographs and maps.

5: The author recommends as the definitive modern work on the West Clare Railway the book *The West Clare Railway* by Patrick Taylor, revised by Allan Baker. It was published by Plateway Press in 1994 as ISBN 1-8719080-16-X, and virtually leaves no stone unturned.

6: Steve Flanders' book *The County Donegal Railway* gives considerable illustrated detail about the railway's locomotives and rolling stock. The book was published in 1996 by Midland Publishing Limited, ISBN 1 85780 054-0.

7: The author's interest in the Irish Turf Board railways has been inspired by the book *Locomotives and Railcars of Bord na Móna* by Stephen Johnson, published in 1996 by Midland Publishing Limited, ISBN 1 85780 045-1. The book details all powered rolling stock, historic and current, and has useful background and contact information, and a location map.

Above: *The Railway Preservation Society of Ireland is naturally international. Based in Whitehead in Northern Ireland and in Mullingar in Eire, the society's members co-operate fully in running special trains across and on both sides of the border. In 1950s CIÉ livery, class J15 0-6-0 No. 184 waits to leave Limerick with a tour train to Tipperary on 14th May 1988.*

❝A LARGE CROWD had gathered on the platforms of Thurles station to see GNR 4-4-0 No. 171 and its railtour train. The locomotive had stopped to take water. As the enthusiasts and local onlookers mingled, a local person was heard to remark in awe: "There are people on this train from England, America and even Belfast!"❞

Irish Railways
1996

Lough Swilly
Portrush
Coleraine
Ballycastle
Ballymoney
Cushendal
Castlerock
Lough Foyle
Londonderry
Letterkenny
Stranorlar
Strabane
Ballymena
Larne
Glenties
Donegal
Cookstown
Antrim
Belfast Lough
Bangor
Killybegs
Lough Neagh
BELFAST
Bundoran
Ballyshannon
Omagh
Lisburn
Fintona
Dungannon
Portadown
Clogher
Armagh
Downpatrick
Manorhamilton
Enniskillen
Keady
Newry
Newcastle
Sligo
Belcoo
Monaghan
Warrenpoint
Collooney
Ballinamore
Clones
Arigna
Belturbet
Castleblaney
Dundalk
Boyle
Ballyhaise
Ballina
Ballaghaderreen
Dromod
Cavan
Kingscourt
Ardee
Carrick-on-Shannon
Oldcastle
Drogheda
Castlebar
Longford
Navan
Westport
Claremorris
Ballinrobe
Roscommon
Mullingar
Tuam
Enfield
Malahide
Howth
Athlone
Edenderry
Maynooth
DUBLIN
Galway
Athenry
Ballinasloe
Clara
Dun Laoghaire
Loughrea
Kildare
Naas
Bray
Banagher
Portarlington
Gort
Birr
Mountmellick
Athy
Wicklow
Ennistymon
Corofin
Port Laoise
Ennis
Nenagh
Roscrea
Abbeyleix
Tullow
Arklow
Milltown Malbay
Ballybrophy
Carlow
Kilkee
Thurles
Gorey
Kilrush
Limerick
Kilkenny
Enniscorthy
Foynes
Limerick Junction
Tipperary
Cashel
New Ross
Wexford
Listowel
Clonmel
Fenit
Tralee
Charleville
Cahir
Waterford
Rosslare Harbour
Dingle
Castleisland
Newmarket
Mallow
Michelstown
Tramore
Farranfore
Fermoy
Dungarvan
Killarney
Banteer
Valentia Harbour
Macroom
Kenmare
Cork
Youghal
Passage
C6bh
Bandon
Bantry
Drimoleague
Clonakilty
Schull
Skibbereen
Courtmacsherry
Baltimore

River Shannon

Key:
Lines open to all traffic:
IÉ
NIR
Lines open to Freight traffic only:
IÉ
NIR
International border · · · · · · · ·

CPB
6-97